A Michael Eigen Companion

I0105075

A Michael Eigen Companion offers 150 essential quotes, carefully selected from Michael Eigen's books, alongside explorative commentary.

An expert on the work of Eigen, Bagai's curated quotes are accompanied by commentary on particular topics to highlight their spiritual, ethical, and psychoanalytic aspects. The excerpts offer moments of psychological "soul wisdom"— gateways for quiet reflection and contemplation. Eigen's ecumenical theoretical approach fosters a humane and relational clinical attitude founded upon respectful care for wounded souls and their capacity for emotional growth and aliveness, even within the depths of psychic injury and despair. Bringing together quotes from Eigen's published work, interviews, and talks, this book provides a distilled guide to his voluminous oeuvre.

At the confluence of psychoanalysis, spirituality, and psychology, *A Michael Eigen Companion* will be indispensable for readers from a wide range of psychoanalytic and spiritual backgrounds. It will also appeal to students of literature and philosophy, Jungians and Buddhists, as well as seekers of psychological and emotional wisdom.

Robin Bagai, Psy.D. is a clinical psychologist in Portland, Oregon, who has been practicing psychoanalytic psychotherapy for over 35 years. His book, *Commentaries on the Work of Michael Eigen* (Routledge), adds to his publications in journals and anthologies. Dr. Bagai has been leading in-person and international seminars on over a dozen of Michael Eigen's books since 2014.

confusion. Eigen's mystical clinical-theoretical touch is artfully illuminated through Bagai's psychoanalytic vision."

Loray Daws, Ph.D., D.Psa, Psychoanalyst
and Clinical Psychologist

"Robin Bagai provides us a gift with this stimulating compendium of Michael Eigen's psychoanalytic insights. Moments that touch spirit and soul from quotes that both edify and enlighten."

Ofra Eshel, faculty, training and supervising analyst,
Israel Psychoanalytic Society; author, *The Emergence of
Analytic Oneness: Into the Heart of Psychoanalysis*

"What a delight it is to meander through the fertile garden of Mike Eigen's enduring and generous testimony to the richness of analytic and lived experience as opened up by the many vivid selections in this book."

Jeffrey Eaton, psychoanalyst and author of
A Fruitful Harvest: Essays after Bion

"Robin Bagai's book is an invitation to know Michael Eigen's work more intimately. It sheds light on Eigen's insights into the conditions, conflicts and inexplicable mystery of being human. And much like Eigen himself, Bagai's book is a wonderful friend and a fantastic teacher."

Selma Duckler, Honorary Member of The American
Psychoanalytic Association

"Through 'Wisdom Moments' Robin Bagai takes the reader on a mystic path along the shadow lines of the human mind

"I am grateful Robin Bagai is sharing aspects of my work touching moments of feeling and reverie that enrich and nourish. His selections increase appreciation of our multi-dimensional existence and deepen a sense of being. Say hello to new and old experiential possibilities and the wonder and care they inspire."

Michael Eigen, Ph.D., author of *The Challenge of Being Human* and *Contact with the Depths*

"Robin Bagai offers a luminous tribute to Michael Eigen. He has carefully and lovingly curated a treasure trove of quotes that throb with feeling, depth, aliveness and Eigen's timeless wisdom. A book to savor, return to, and be transformed by."

Shalini Masih, United Kingdom, Psychotherapist and Author, *Psychoanalytic Conversations with States of Spirit Possession: Beauty in Brokenness*

"Robin Bagai has accomplished an impossible feat, hand-selecting some of Eigen's most memorable quotes, a creative task in itself. The book reads like mantras, each to be meditated upon, opening up new spheres of experience."

Joon ho Lee, Korean translator for Michael Eigen's Seminars in Seoul 1,2,3, and Director of the Korean Institute for Contemporary Psychoanalysis

"In this Eigen Companion, Robin Bagai enlivens what companioning could mean in many of Michael Eigen's works: honoring the spirit, listening to the heart, bearing witness by walking alongside, cultivating stillness, discovering the gift of sacred silence, and partnering disorder, if not fertile

to come out eager and in love with Eigen's oeuvre and psychoanalysis."

Shifa Haq, Psychoanalytic Psychotherapist and Assistant Professor, Ambedkar University Delhi. Author of *In Search of Return— Mourning the Disappearances in Kashmir*

"In this book Robin Bagai brings together 150 quotations that have accompanied the prolific psychoanalyst Michael Eigen in and out of the consulting room. Displaying knowledge, respect, and affection for Eigen, he transports us with gentleness and fearlessness into the depths of Eigen's work. The result is a unique collection in which each quote has a life of its own; the author turns the reading into an eloquent transformative experience. This book is an extraordinary contribution to the great themes of contemporary psychoanalysis."

Jani Santamaría, PhD, co-editor of *The Bion Seminars at the A-Santamaría Association* and editor of *Bion, Dreamwork and the Oneiric Dimensions of the Mind* (both Routledge)

"It is Michael Eigen's compassion for his fellow human beings that is the foundation of his many achievements. Robin Bagai gives us a sample of the thoughts this compassion engendered by carefully culling one hundred and fifty remarkable quotes from Michael Eigen's books, a daunting task that Bagai nevertheless manages to complete successfully. This collection of quotes will be welcome to those who are very familiar with Eigen's work and to those who are not."

Thomas R. Federn, New York City; grandson of Paul Federn, a founding member of Freud's Viennese Psychoanalytic Society

EDITED BY ROBIN BAGAI

A Michael Eigen Companion
Moments of Wisdom from a Psychoanalytic Mystic

Routledge
Taylor & Francis Group

LONDON AND NEW YORK

Designed cover image: Getty | ChaNaWiT

First published 2026
by Routledge
4 Park Square, Milton Park, Abingdon, Oxon OX14 4RN

and by Routledge
605 Third Avenue, New York, NY 10158

Routledge is an imprint of the Taylor & Francis Group, an informa business

For Product Safety Concerns and Information please contact our EU representative
GPSR@taylorandfrancis.com. Taylor & Francis Verlag GmbH, Kaufingerstraße 24,
80331 München, Germany.

British Library Cataloguing-in-Publication Data
A catalogue record for this book is available from the British Library

ISBN: 9781032987743 (hbk)
ISBN: 9781032987729 (pbk)
ISBN: 9781003600480 (ebk)

DOI: 10.4324/9781003600480

Typeset in Joanna MT
by codeMantra

To soul keepers and spirit seekers everywhere,
and to those lonely and forlorn wandering deserts
of the digital twenty-first century

Contents

Contents

"... more important than ever now ..."

Michael Eigen uses these words in a quote Robin Bagai includes in this book: "Movement through injury and recovery is part of our psychic pulse, a basic rhythm, more important than ever now, when there are mounting fears (again) that disaster has the last word." (2005, p. 61) "... Mounting fears (again) that disaster has the last word" is an emotional experience shared by many people in the world today. We seem to be creating external catastrophes in our shortcoming to evolve as a species, situated in a position between the finite and the infinite, with a capacity for awareness of both. Wilfred Bion exposed, in the context of the relationship of container and contained, the individual and his relationship to the group, an enormous anxiety in our make-up towards experiencing genuine developmental change. There is a "tendency," as Donald Meltzer paraphrases, "for change to manifest itself as catastrophe"; it is dreaded. The dread arises in our contact with reality, which "is not something which lends itself to be known," as Bion puts it.

What shape does human subjectivity take, then? Can we survive ourselves with such anxiety in our make-up? How? This is one important thrust in Eigen's work. The responses in his conceptualizations, clinical work, and style of writing are notably aesthetic in nature. Eigen is a musician as well as a psychoanalyst. He studied literature in college. I believe his encounter with reality is mainly poietic. Eigen 'heard' through Bion's work and others', something else that is in our make-up: a basic rhythm of breakdown and recovery, and of rebirth, which he also calls a "rhythm of faith". This basic rhythm is a part of our poietic capacity. Eigen's work can be seen as a blossom of the "aesthetic development" in psychoanalysis that Meg Harris Williams brought out. Eigen opens fields of experience, along with new dimensions and possibilities of growth—where contact with the unknowable, experiencing psychic pain, dread, madness, emotional storms, beauty, and a "boundless unknown support" can become more tolerable. His literary style of writing is especially effective as a conduit in transmission of meaning. Many of the quotes in this book convey vistas of a human subjectivity more resilient to catastrophe, its challenges, and aspects of our destructiveness in hatred of reality. I think the collection of curated quotes in this book is a companion more important than ever now.

Bagai has been studying Eigen's work over many years. He has travelled the length and breadth of Eigen's oeuvre, and has taught many of his books in weekly seminars for a decade. His selection of Eigen quotes in this book takes the reader through many façades of our being with gentle, mostly silent, company. This is a sense I know from Bagai's seminars as well, his humble company in sharing the richness of Eigen's work that he has assimilated over the years. In this book, the depth of his knowledge of Eigen's work is seen in his selection of quotes. They reflect both many of the essential aspects of Eigen's work and provide momentary sources of reflection, wisdom, and insight. With some of these, Bagai draws attention to the "intrinsic pain of life," as well as "the fire that never goes out," an "intimate presence," and a "deeper love." Some of the quotes underline the significance of "making room for insufficiency," that integrity is not wholeness, that totalitarianism is a word derived from "total," and there is creative potential in accepting limitation. Faith, waiting, and toleration of the unknown are some of the capacities emphasized. The quotes recurrently touch on mystery; they speak of spontaneity and joy of life; they explore living together with insoluble conflicts. One of the themes is our challenge of "surviving aliveness," surviving psyche's pressures, the impact of reality. Our insufficiency in that regard is so real and touching that it immediately evokes mercy for oneself and others, if not the opposite, "hatred in response to deficit." Eigen's words organically pull one more towards the former as they nourish the mind and soul and pave a way toward deep integrations.

Bagai's approach to sharing Eigen's work in this book reminds me of Turkish architect and scholar Doğan Kuban's translation of the *Tao Te Ching* to Turkish after 65 years of reading and studying it, with brief interpretations inserted. Bagai's commentaries in this book are fewer in number, he is more of a silent companion, but the significant plainness in presentation is similar. With gaps provided allowing readers to breathe, I think this is a just approach to sharing the work, for, in terms of intensity, Eigen's passages are often comparable to Lao Tzu's. Presenting Eigen's work in this way, Bagai also amplifies the vibrancy and poetic quality of Eigen's writing. He suggests the quotes in this book can best be read randomly, without seeking a systematic unfolding. Such a reading is fecund for readers' own creations of meaning and semantic interweaving among the quotes.

I hope readers will savor, in these times and beyond, the thoughtful, respectful company of this invaluable collection of Eigen quotes by Bagai.

Izmir, Turkey
March 2025

Preface and Acknowledgements

I have long been bewildered by the impression that Michael Eigen's work is better known and loved outside the United States than within his native New York. I don't know if this is accurate or not, but I often joke with colleagues here in the western US that Eigen is one of the few psychologists with over 30 books to his name that no one has ever heard of.

The idea for this book came about as a way to enhance Eigen's visibility by putting together a hand-picked compendium of his remarkable quotes—moments of quiet and uncanny wisdom that shed new light on contemporary psychology and psychotherapy. I make no claim that these are his "best" quotes, only that they stopped me in my tracks, stunned my psyche, and made me think, feel, and weep as much as great novels often do. Eigen believes that fiction is often truer and more real than non-fiction because it portrays and evokes what is closest to us—our emotional life and experiential reality.

In these pages you will find insightful moments that ring true in the same deep way that profound dreams can—wisdom-moments that touch heart and guts, soul and spirit, using only the written word. But these are words that speak from their own insides and somehow find their way inside ours. It has been a labor of love to mine these glistening sparks and nuggets from Eigen's work over the past 15 years, and I hope they nourish all who feel starved for what seems increasingly absent today: a sensitive caring for humanity and what is psychologically real, including our painful and destructive truths.

This book would not have happened without much ongoing international support from colleagues who have attended my online seminars and encouraged me to pursue such a book. But my chief supporter and biggest encourager has been my life partner, Willa, a poet and psychotherapist herself. She helped make this work possible through our mutual daily resonance of creative effort and committed practice, and I could not have done it without her grounding presence and loving kindness.

Internationally, there are too many people to thank, so I am sending gratitude to all of you in your representative countries, including Canada, Mexico, Brazil, Argentina, the UK, Germany, Slovenia, Israel, Turkey, India, Korea, Northern Ireland, Sweden, Jordan, Australia, New Zealand, South Africa, Italy, Spain, and Georgia, as well as the United States. I hold much gratitude and appreciation for all of you who remain silently present within these pages. You know who you are, and who you continue to be—part of a generative world community of sensitive selves who carry forward and guard the inner life of psyche.

Finally, I want to thank the kind, attentive, hardworking people at Routledge, Taylor & Francis. In particular, Susannah Frearson, Saloni Singhania, and copy-editor Yvonne Doney— for their many efforts on behalf of this book, for continuing to extend the reach of Michael Eigen's work, and for seeing value in presenting these excerpts in this particular format. A deep bow to all.

DEAR READER,

This is a book of quintessential quotes from the work of Michael Eigen—a companion for those seeking psychological and spiritual wisdom. It is a book meant to provide moments of brief immersion that deepen into reflection and pondering. Much like a *Book of Hours* or words from ancient Chinese philosophers such as Lao Tzu or Chuang Tzu, this book can be opened at random to any page where one will find quiet prayers and poems of illumination flashing wisdom of psyche and emotional truth. Strictly speaking, there are no "poems" in this collection, but there are psychological "psalms" and meditations drawn from the heart of joy, wonder, despair, and amazement at what it means to be a human being.

Michael Eigen is a psychologist and psychoanalyst with more than six decades of clinical practice and over 30 published books. This curated collection from his oeuvre continues to hold moments of fresh impact for me—even many years after first encountering them. Eigen has sometimes called himself a psychoanalytic mystic, and his book bearing that title (1998) is an early collection of essays that transport the reader to diverse realms of psycho-spiritual meaning, often with simultaneous experiential probes.

DOI: 10.4324/9781003600480-1

Having spent time with Eigen at his Manhattan office as well as walking with him around Park Slope, sharing dinners, stage plays, and jogging together in Brooklyn's Prospect Park, I feel at liberty to describe him and his writing as an enigmatic composite: part Taoist sage, part Western mystic, part psychoanalytic rebel, part kabbalistic tzaddik ... with many parts remaining unknown—as private and sacred as Winnicott's *incommunicado core*.

The reader may wonder why psychoanalysis and mysticism appear together, as they seem to be rather strange bedfellows. One might describe psychoanalysis, when stripped bare, as two people meeting regularly and often to discuss the life of an analysand *vis-a-vis* inner workings of head, heart, soul, and gut. Over its relatively short lifetime psychoanalysis has given birth to many schools and techniques, many methods and orientations, and, like psyche herself, it never rests. Both theory and practice continue to evolve and grow. There are many branches of the psychoanalytic tree now, some more codified and manualized, others freer and more spontaneous (along with many mixtures). But whatever the school or orientation, clinical practice relies upon the value of a consistent frame within which a wide array of human gravitas takes place. And in every school and orientation, each comes up against the limits and power of *mystery* to greater or lesser degrees, much as Freud pondered the navel of the dream disappearing into unknown meaning (*unerkannten*).

Perhaps the reader can already sense mystery in my joining together unlike things (e.g., variety within consistency; codified yet spontaneous). Metaphor itself is a creative mystery— forming new meaning from mixing unlike things. Michael Eigen uses metaphor, mystery, and paradox, among others, to shed new light on human psychology and emotional reality. His books such as *Toxic Nourishment* and *Damaged Bonds* sit side-by-side with others titled *The Sensitive Self, Faith,* and *The Challenge of Being Human.*

Part of the allure and intrigue of psychoanalysis in any form is its abiding interest in our unconscious mind—the name we give to that unknown and mysterious part or process of the mind that is partly awake while we sleep, and barely sleeps when we're awake. At times, our unconscious serves as sentinel and protector. At other times it opens treasure chests of intimations, barely discernible. The unconscious mind is often said to be the birthplace of new ideas and imagination, but, when damaged, it can also function as a lure towards entropy, deadness, and destruction.

What is this mysterious part of us? A wellspring of potential growth from depths of unknown processes? A seething cauldron of psychic energy? An unfathomably obscure domain, closer to ourselves than we know?

We don't know … and to make matters worse, the unconscious mind is apparently not just one thing. The phrase itself can function as a noun, adjective or adverb. The name or label we give it means precisely this: we-don't-know-what-this-is. Yet more than glimpses are found through dreams, slips of the tongue, accidents, synchronies, visions, archetypes, paradox, impulse, intuition, madness, and artistic achievement. The unconscious as conceived today in the West is a mystery far greater than Freud's (repressed) unconscious. Its living history is partly represented by a wide variety of traditions, including the work of Carl Jung, ancient Sanskrit texts, Buddhist sutras, zen koans, Kabbalah, Sufi writings, and Gnosticism, to name a few.

I like to think of our unconscious mind resembling a continuously pregnant void, a fecund inchoate emptiness … ever self-renewing, ever being born, and ever cycling through mini deaths and alive awakenings. This unknown yet ever evolving essence serves as the foundation of our psychic life.

In this volume I have chosen a selection of significant passages from Michael Eigen's body of work. My aim was to collect the most resonant and edifying excerpts that swim at the confluence of psyche and spirit, emotional experience and living truth, capturing both beauty and destruction dancing among their many cousins who, at different moments, hold hands, fight, make up, kiss, and tyrannize one another.

The reader is encouraged to open the book at random, spending time with each quote rather than seek any systematic unfolding, because nothing of that sort exists. Michael Eigen's work is diverse and ecumenical, addressing universal human concerns, the foundation of which consists of mind/body relations in concert with one's experience of self and others—all of which evolve as a complex mixture from birth and before. While such a grand amalgam can never be captured in its entirety, Eigen's droplets of spiritual and emotional truth continue to nourish many, as I hope they will you.

> It is part of emotional life that we can express or narrate or convey only a bit of what we feel. We do not know the whole of it. There is always some frustration built in. It is like swimming in the ocean. We can never take in the whole ocean all at once. But we do swim in part of it and the water we swim in, while not the whole ocean, is real water.
>
> (2011a, p. 124)

If, as Carl Jung declared, psychology is a subjective confession, herein lies a collection of thoughts and feelings subject to personal taste. It is a taste of inner life, conveyed with an experiential "feel" that resonates with deep wisdom, acknowledging many facets of our all-too-human condition. For some, a certain openness and suspension of disbelief will help, especially those new to Eigen's work. For others, it may feel as though his words are speaking to you from inside yourself.

My study of Eigen's work over many years has allowed for prolonged incubation, leading to my book of *Commentaries* (2023) on two of his major works. This in turn was the result of having taught over a dozen of his books in weekly seminars since 2014. I hope to have several of these lecture series available for viewing online in 2026.

Lecturing on Eigen's work over the years, it felt as though an underground mycelium was growing, revealing ever-unfolding connected roots as vast as Indra's celestial net. Eventually, sustained openness and receptivity brought forth a flow of glowing sparks, colorful mushrooms and shooting stars, combining fertile subsoil with cosmic dust that asked for a dreamcatcher's net to express soul intimacy through words. But for this book, rather than finding new words, I've decided to catch a variety of the dream fish already alive and swimming in Eigen's ocean.

Most of the quoted excerpts in this book stand on their own—some as psychoanalytic koans, some as naked emotional truth, some as prayers, and some as spiritual callings to try to grow our humanity—imploring us to mix our longings for a saner world with growth of capacity for walking in each other's shoes, and walking in our own shoes more fully. A smaller portion of excerpts have begged for annotation, and for those I provide some context and commentary. My intention is always in service of adding to and illuminating Michael Eigen's thoughts and ideas ... if only a little. I hope the reader will benefit as much as I have.

Portland, Oregon
March 2025

HOLINESS

My sense of the holy has a positive and a negative source. The positive is the holiness of life and of human life. The negative is the awakening that comes from seeing the inevitability of injury and the wish to work with, struggle with our nature. The holiness of therapy involves, in part, a practical application of this struggle with life to release life, to make life better. With me, the sense of holiness also has a sense of feeling free, connected, home: working with the human psyche as a kind of home. An odd kind of home, since we don't feel at home there, a homeless home. But home none the less.

(2007a, Epigraph)

* * * * *

Eigen offers a credo at the confluence of two rivers: suffering and psychological growth. A call to and from psyche, our homeless home. Addressing the inevitability of injury, we struggle with ourselves and our nature in an attempt to make life better—an eternal challenge never more poignant than today.

DOI: 10.4324/9781003600480-2

BEAUTY AND ETHICS

Beauty, I believe, is one source of ethics. To see something beautiful can arouse a sense of goodness. Not only a sense of feeling good, but also a sense of wanting to do right by, wanting to do justice to, a world which can be so beautiful, which can so touch one to the depths.

(2014b, p. 1)

WONDER, AWE AND NOT-KNOWING

Where does the experience of no knowing or not knowing or "I don't know" take you? What does it open? How many of us, how often, and how deeply dwell with this elusive but fecund sense? In childhood, we tease our minds and souls with not knowing who we are or how we got here— anything, everything, the whole universe, life itself, why here, this way? We tease ourselves into oblivion, wonder, and awe and shudder at the discovery of thrills and frights not mentioned by anyone we know, pleasures of going further and further into unknown, nameless whirls, pools within pools ... dizzying and unfathomable.

(2011a, p. 50)

ETHICS OF THE UNKNOWN

There is an ethics of the unknown. An attitude of unknowing leaves things open, protects against false omniscience. In an argument with your partner you may be convinced that you are right, the other wrong. It is commonplace to blame the other, exonerate the self. The reverse also is not unusual. Aggression turns against the other and/or the self. If we assimilate the fact that we do not know everything about ourselves and the other and that, like the universe, we are mostly unknown to ourselves, a sense of humility and openness may have a chance to grow. We may become more interested in learning more about who we are and readying for further development. This is an entirely different attitude than slamming the door with dogma.

(2016b, pp. 19–20)

SENSITIVITY AND ETHICS

In psychoanalysis, we learn a little more about destruction. We learn, or think we learn, that feelings matter, that we are sensitive beings who need to sense how sensitivity works, that ethics has roots in sensitivity to ourselves and others.

(2014b, p. 7)

WORDLESS IMMENSITY

Overwhelming immensity of the wordless. Words are like ants biting and chewing bits off immensity. Beginningless immensity that words never catch up with, that words help to create. Immensity on the one hand, hole on the other ... Superabundance, deficit, impoverishment. Hyper-plus, zero, hyper-minus. Emotional flooding and emptying, rise and fall of feeling. We dream of being overcome by ocean waves because we can drown, because another person can overwhelm us, because we breathe feeling as well as air.

(2007b, p. 37)

* * * * *

We breathe feelings as well as air—a truth hiding in plain sight. Eigen here offers hints of profound parallels between our physical and psychological beings.

AWESOME LIVING BEING

It is awesome to be a living being who feels, cries, laughs, sings, dies. Who hurts others and is hurt, who goes mad, becomes inspired, or is just happy to be alive to each day to the extent one can. Life never ceases being an unpredictable sea, raising up, dashing down, pressing us through ranges of emotions, more alive, threatened, empty, deadened, eager.

(2011a, p. xiii)

KNOWLEDGE AND BEING

After many years of therapy, a "hard-core resistant" patient might say, "I know all this. How does it help? I'm just the same." In such a case, therapy did not manage to break out of the knowledge game. Knowing or insight is not enough. A change of *being* is necessary.

One has to get underneath knowing and make contact with *experiencing*. Knowledge is important as a scaffolding, a frame of reference.

But it must function as a bridge or link or jump-off point for further experiencing. There is a subtle interplay between experiencing and knowledge. To an important extent, the quality of experiencing gets fine tuning from the breadth, depth, and subtlety of knowledge available. If one is in touch with experience, the more one knows the better. But if the link is broken, one goes round in circles.

(1992, p. 39, original emphasis)

* * * * *

After more than a century of development, the tree of psychoanalysis has undergone much growth. Two branches of this tree might be described as "Knowledge" and "Being," or theory and felt sense … understanding and lived-experience … insight and impact. Each domain sits underneath its respective philosophical umbrella of epistemology and ontology. While these two remain forever intertwined, one's approach as a therapist often rests on assumptions that lean more toward one path or another: cognitive insight and understanding, or relational growth of impact leading to experiential opening of psyche and person.

Generally speaking, early analysts viewed the mind as an apparatus for thinking and believed that knowledge, insight and understanding led to "cure." For Winnicott, Bion, and Eigen, "experiencing one's experience" and the impact of both conscious and unconscious relational exchange as catalysts for growth took on increasing importance. Likewise, personal development that furthers aliveness for living life began to supersede notions of conflict resolution and cure. So-called one-person and two-person therapy models can, in part, be traced to how one uses these tree branches. But why should these dear ancestral relatives, forever sitting side by side, still be stuck in turf battles rather than dancing arm in arm? Reluctant twinships ever in need of imaginative ways to bridge philosophies of the natural and human sciences.

A CIRCLE WE MUST LIVE WITH

Jung wrote that psychology is a subjective confession; every mental act has its own perspective. If science tries to account for consciousness, it can only do so through consciousness. This is a circle we must live with ... Consciousness is both subject and object to itself, yet it needs to transcend itself as well.

(2018b, p. 21)

* * * * *

There is no Archimedean point outside consciousness from which to obtain "objective" views of consciousness. We are always on the inside ... forever within consciousness. Even when self-reflection occurs, it is part of the circle. This is one of the great paradoxes of conscious life. We are both a subjective experiential flow and an object for self-reflection.

When scientists study patterns in nature or physicians study the human body, regularity and predictability advance our knowledge of the physical material world. But who can say what dreams we might have tonight, or why we fall in love with this particular person and not another?

THE BRAIN AND EXPERIENCE

It is becoming more common today to think that brain and experience are not simply two terms split off from or reducible to one another, but rather that they may be viewed as entering into a mutually constitutive relationship. Each sets requirements that dictate the structural possibilities of the other. Our understanding of the mutual influence of brain and experience is in its infancy.

(2018b, p. 22)

* * * * *

It is no surprise that experiences we undergo in life cause changes to brain and nervous system, most pronounced during infancy. Yet the particular impact of this or that experience is neither foreseeable nor universal, as people have a wide range of response capacity to the same event. One person will suffer shock and immobilization after an earthquake, while another might leap into reparative action, helping others.

Our thoughts and beliefs themselves can alter the body's physical and chemical processes, as evidenced by the placebo effect, a continuing mystery that necessitates double-blind studies in medication trials to ascertain validity and reliability.

The brain is a fluid organ and our experiences even more so—both are complex interconnected mysteries, and mystery is an essential ingredient in psyche's evolution. Consider a thought experiment: the scientific goal of eventually having "complete" knowledge of the brain—which, according to laws of the physical sciences, would mean elements of prediction and control. If we suppose this is attainable, wouldn't it, paradoxically, end innovation, imagination, and creative development?

To paraphrase W.R. Bion: the principles of psychic development are unknown …

Shouldn't we add brain development as well? Our material and experiential "brains" are intertwined and forever influencing one another. Scientists may be able to map components of the brain and nervous system, but, alongside these fluid systems of synaptic interaction percolates experiential reality—ever evolving with unknown potentials, including unknown unknowns and, disconcertingly, unknowable unknowns, much to our ego's chagrin.

EVOLUTION OF EXPERIENCE

As in all my work, my desire is not to "solve" anything, but to open fields of experiencing ... My work asks, simply, give experience a chance. It is enough to try to stay with some bits of experience and see where they take us. W. R. Bion's work, like John Dewey's or Alfred North Whitehead's, each in their ways, is about enduring the capacity to experience, partnering this capacity, evolving with it ...

It is different from a "bully model". It practices resisting the urge to bully experience (it endures this urge, experiences it).

(2007a, pp. 130–32)

* * * * *

When psychotherapy is at its best, we participate in the evolution of personal experience. Greater capacity for experiencing life allows more freedom to choose from life's possibilities, and more possibilities allow more engagement with living life. A virtuous circle of unfolding.

The simple words opening and closing point to psychological dynamics of great importance. When we are open to life and experience, we are receptive, permeable, non-defensive, engaged ... and, at the same time, more vulnerable to being hurt.

When closed, we are more or less shut off, protected, armored, invulnerable ... and, at the same time, less available for contact with life, self, and others. One direction expands life's reach accompanied by risk, the other forecloses out of need for safety.

Eigen reminds us that psychoanalysis is partly a compendium of ways we try to escape from ourselves. To touch an inner pain point brings recoil, contraction similar to touching a sea anemone. To work with pain involves a practice of shared pain-touching. Better outcomes consist of more tolerance and growth of capacity to work with pain points so they don't rule our lives. With care and respect, over time, such work can bring about less recoil and contraction from our emotional sea anemones.

HEALTH AND SUFFERING

Thinking you have to be [emotionally] healthy is one of the great diseases of our time.

(2007a, p. 66)

* * * * *

A key phrase and red flag: "have to ..." A command from an inner tyrant's voice, insisting on what "must" or "should be."

Rigid goals drawn from idealization or totalizing thinking conjures inflexible attitudes that run counter to psychical and emotional health.

What exactly does it mean to be emotionally healthy? Is this idealized, as in "perfectly healthy"? Do you know anyone who is? Or do we think of health as merely the absence of symptoms? What if suffering itself is part of a well-rounded healthy emotional life? Consider the following:

Psychoanalysis often says that increased capacity for contact involves increased ability to undergo suffering ... For example, Winnicott (1988) writes, "Probably the greatest suffering in the human world is the suffering of the normal or healthy or mature person." Suffering is part of health. The more psyche, the more suffering. One makes oneself smaller to avoid pain.

A corollary to the idea that one curtails development in order to avoid suffering is: the more one cares, the more open to suffering one becomes. One truncates caring to downplay pain.

(2007b, p. 31)

MASTERY AND MYSTERY

The realization that we can never fully possess ourselves (or anything) leads us to explore the *aesthetics of openness*. We become artists of non-possessiveness, adept at permitting experiencing to build and speak. We learn to listen and reply. We become partners with our athletic drive toward mastery and the plenitude of unknowing, our need to control and our need to be reborn through mystery. Mastery and mystery—double poles of our nature. We have an infinite hunger for both.

(2018b, p. 249, my emphasis)

HORIZON OF HUMILITY

We will not rid ourselves of our make-up but, one hopes, learn to work with it a little better, become better partners with our capacities. At the same time, all of our studies of "higher" or "lower" end capacities have roots in the vast unknown, supernal and subtending. Our pleasure and pride in exercising our capacities must take place within a greater horizon of humility.

(2014c, p. 39)

OUR MAD PSYCHE

Our mad psyche is permeated by idealizing tendencies, a sense of purity, a sense of beauty. So much that ennobles us, that lifts life and fills it with color and makes it worthwhile, adds to human madness and misery. We are quite mad. Even our sanity is dangerous. The link between sanity, sanitize, sanitation, cleaning up your act, is a wish to somehow get out of our messy plight. In *Emotional Storm* (2005a), I try to show that we need to get used to our upheaval, learn to work within the storm ...

Getting out of it, rising above it does not seem to do the trick. We need to enlarge processes of receptivity to become better storm partners, storm processors.

(2007a, p. 64)

ABSOLUTE STATES AND POSSESSIVENESS

Many moments in life are absolutized. Mystical states, falling in love, religious belief, devotion to a cause, ideology, leader. A sense of *one*: there is only *one* college to go to, *one* person to be with, *one* way of being a psychoanalyst, *one* way to love God. Often it is *my* one at the expense of *yours*. One and possessiveness go together.

(2007b, p. 54, original emphasis)

* * * * *

To fully possess or be absolutely certain, to have definitive answers or think we know what's best for others, is often arrogant and foolhardy. Even when we give our best efforts, they must arise within a context of humility for our limited perspective and all that remains outside our purview.

MUTUAL CORRECTIVENESS

It is hard to say, but we would not be who we are without madness, any more than we would be who we are without death. We would be poorer without its truths and contradictions. But we must fight to get to a place where the mutual correctiveness of seemingly exclusive viewpoints, worlds, experiential capacities, and strategies is possible. We must keep getting to places where mutual correctiveness can become a way of life. This means not only fidelity to one's own vision, but also fidelity to the impact of the vision of others. We live in a cauldron of seething possibilities. It is doubtful that madness can be eliminated any more than death can. But we can seek an attitude large enough and open enough to encompass it. We can learn from it and treat it as a partner in evolution.

(2018b, p. 370)

* * * * *

Here, Eigen offers a template for remaining open to the importance of other worlds and viewpoints so that we don't become stuck in rigid, one-sided attitudes and beliefs. Circumstances are always changing and contexts are innumerable.

A MIX OF INFINITIES

Faith mingles with catastrophe, a mix of infinities. One infinity limits another. Catastrophic dread may be part of processes that destroy personality, but it also can help keep personality honest.

Faith can elevate or sweeten existence, but may suffocate curiosity. How a capacity contributes to or impedes growth is an open matter. There is no substitute for fresh exercise of one's equipment in the moment at hand.

(2004[1993], p. 265)

PSYCHIC BINOCULARITY

Part of psychic binocularity is to fuse or integrate images of health and trauma—one eye on injury, one on recovery and growth, although they work together, often seamlessly.

A vehicle that makes room for double-seeing is faith. (Wilfred) Bion describes faith as an open attitude, open to O. It includes sensitive openness to impacts of reality and generative working with those impacts. The freedom (unbinding) of faith is, partly, a response to the binding of disaster. Faith meets catastrophe and supports personal resilience. Myths and religions echo this movement in terms of death and resurrection, transformation, rebirth, re-finding and renewal. Movement through injury and recovery is part of our psychic pulse, a basic rhythm, more important than ever now, when there are mounting fears (again) that disaster has the last word.

(2005a, pp. 60–1)

ON HIERARCHY

One of the great contributions of modern cultural history is to question the basis of traditional hierarchies, perhaps the very meaning of hierarchy (top–bottom). In psychic realities double arrows are placed between traditional oppositions. What a relief to be able to flow back and forth between antagonistic currents and not pit one against the other. One takes and learns from each. Each contributes to the growth of self. Without polarities life would be poorer, but we do not have to be trapped by polarities. Our model now is paradoxical–dialectical–dialogical (conflict is a branch) ... I think we have very exciting journeys ahead if we do not kill each other off with polemics and prejudice.

(2004[1993], p. 266)

ON SELF-DESTRUCTION

Some feel we are trying to eradicate ourselves in order to solve the problem of being human. Most of us prefer a less dramatic solution. The latter may require us to build more of a taste for the unsolvable and appreciate a little movement at a time. Can we become a little less harmful to others and ourselves? ... I see this as an evolutionary challenge.

(2014c, p. 21)

We need to study the ways we destroy ourselves. We need university courses, perhaps departments, on self-destruction. This is something all the peoples of the world have to

pool knowledge about, and more than knowledge,
have to do something about.

(2007a, p. 54)

* * * * *

*What we do with the destructive sides of our nature is an urgent and
abiding question given the ever-increasing and more powerful weapons
at the world's disposal.*

*Eigen differentiates between forms of psychical destruction and emo-
tional murder used in the service of growth, and concrete physical murder
and destruction that ends life or irreparably damages it.*

*The following series of quotes attend to nuances of both psychical
and physical destructiveness within different contexts. Whereas D.W.
Winnicott's object usage involves "destruction" of projections in
order to become and feel more real, Wilfred Bion wrote of destructiveness
as an independent force in its own right, able to continue destroying ad
infinitum, from and within its own momentum.*

CAN LIFE SURVIVE ITSELF?

One reason Winnicott does not emphasize a
death drive is because the life drive wreaks
enough havoc. An important theme: can
life survive itself? Life itself has destructive
tendencies—territoriality, possessiveness, the
assertion of me over you, not just survival but
domination, triumph, lust for power. We kill to
live. We do not have to go to a death drive to
see how life-affirming tendencies destroy life.
We do not know what to do with the destructive
forces of our life drive, let alone a death drive.

Destructiveness is part of pleasure, exercise
of elan, vitality. Aliveness destroys; aliveness is
dangerous. We do not know what to do with our
aliveness.

(2014b, p. 27)

DESTRUCTIVENESS ITSELF

The vision of destructiveness (like
destructiveness itself) can never be fully
integrated, transformed, metabolized, processed,
converted into something useful. Our ability to
injure ourselves and others never ends. It is cruel
to rationalize all destructiveness as secretly
useful, as hidden good. I think we must make
room for the possibility of destructiveness as
such. Making room is not indulgence. Making
room for the possibility of really being destructive
without precociously rationalizing it, makes room
for spontaneous growth of protective measures.
If one confesses one's viral (virulent) self, one's
touch may soften.

This is not a matter of saying "I'm sorry, I'll be
good," nor a matter of making resolutions. One
knows such attempts spiral out. Being touched
by vision of destructiveness (one's own, others',
life's, the broader currents one is part of), cuts
one to the core, makes one less hardhearted ...
Facing one's destructiveness is no immunization,
but it gives one a different smile and glance, a
different "feel."

(1998, p. 103)

In therapy, we trace murderous impulses, see how they move, work, the forms they take, how they function, what they contribute to the psyche as a whole. Self-destruction and mutual destruction cannot be written off as by-products of attachment difficulties, although the latter can intensify them. They seem ingrained in human nature, a part of who we are. What we do with the destructive side of our nature is an open question. As of now, for the most part, we do not know what to do with it, and making believe we have answers postpones fuller struggles with the question. Jesus comes closest when he says, "Forgive them, father. They don't know what they're doing." We do not know what we are doing and pretending we do compounds the problem.

(2014b, pp. 5–6)

CREATIVE MURDER

We need to survive each other's destructiveness to feel fully alive, part of learning how to live together. To some people killing and being killed comes naturally. They bob up after intense interactions ready for more, as if the risk of undoing each other adds to life. For many, the sense of creative murder does not develop well. They withdraw or become too aggressive, expecting neither self nor other to survive or survive fully. Energetic interactions are costly and traumatizing. The knack or "feel" of coming through each other's impacts needs nurturing.

(2004, pp. 30–31)

The attitude that opens itself to murder Bion calls faith. I think this faith has in it a love of life. It is passionate about living. It opens the heart wide and cannot stop opening. It is a faith that is stronger than murder, that makes murder fruitful.

(2004, p. 35)

PSYCHIC DESTRUCTION AS FREEING

Practice in psychic destruction is freeing, if one "catches on" to the sequence, murder–survival, linked with resilience and responsiveness. Literal murder stops the process, a premature closing. It ends the possibility of letting experience build. What is at stake is the capacity to experience, to be partners with one's capacity to enable experience to develop. The destruction–responsiveness Winnicott speaks of are psychic events, parts of psychic processes. We need to develop the kind of psyche that can experience its destructive urges as expressions of living reality, potentially bringing new forms of intimacy and use of feeling interchange.

(2014b, p. 35)

REALNESS AND MYSTERY

We are all the more real because we are mostly unknown ...

(2016b, p. 8)

* * * * *

An unlikely pair: realness and the unknown. Why these two together? And why is one cast in terms of the other? Is this a psychoanalytic koan? A mystical conundrum?

Wilfred Bion opined that the principles of psychical growth remain unknown. Isn't it a basic thrust of being human to unfold in new and surprising ways? Another thought experiment: if in some future universe there were no unknown parts of psyche... if we never discovered or were surprised by ourselves, wouldn't growth come to a halt?

Asian cultures sometimes speak of unsprouted or "uncooked" seeds within us (karmic or otherwise). I picture this as an ovarian model, keeping reality fresh with as-yet unknown possibilities.

FEELING NORMAL, FEELING ALIVE

Some people never quite feel alive. Others never feel fully normal. Most people suffer such feelings in private. Others may feel deadened all life-long. Eigen asks: why should feeling alive feel normal? His words awaken us to the preciousness of human life in and beyond our ephemeral earthly existence.

* * * * *

What is normal about feeling alive ...? [... It] may never feel normal to be alive. How normal is aliveness in the universe? How normal is the universe? To be a universe is something very special, and to be alive in it even more special. It is not a chance given to everything everywhere.

(1999, p. 108)

BEYOND REPARATION

Both Winnicott and Bion have gone farther than Melanie Klein's depiction of reparation. It's not that reparation isn't real, making up for your bad things. Winnicott is saying that reparation is not the thread he is interested in. That is not the spontaneous thread from the vital spark, from the going on being, through the transitional object, through the use of object. No. He is saying there is another thread, which is not about being guilty and making up for feeling guilty. There is another kind of spontaneity. Another *joie de vivre* that comes out of an élan, a feeling of a joy in life ... He is tracing a spontaneous thread of life that needs support. We have a chance to let this spontaneous life thread grow with every interaction we have.

(2010, p. 71)

ACTUAL AND IDEAL SATISFACTION

We do not know the origins of the link between actual and ideal satisfaction. Perhaps we can say that a memory of ideal satisfaction is some sort of act of imagination. This ideal antedates superego ideals. It is built into the fabric of human pleasure, including use of elemental sensations. Addiction to sensations means addiction to an imaginary state.

Freud's pleasure-ego or ideal ego extends this line of thinking to the ego itself. The ego is addicted to itself as its own ideal. It tries to maintain itself as an ideal state that seeks ideal states. Breaking into this scenario is the ubiquitous threat of pain and insufficiency ... But why we should be creatures who hunger for ideal

satisfaction, not mere satisfaction, remains a
mystery.

(2004[1993], pp. 267–8)

* * * * *

*We measure life against our imagination and often come up short. It
may be impossible to live without the tension and contrast between what
is and what might be. Ideals are unavoidably embedded inside the gap of
our "comparison mind." Might we use this tension as a generative ful-
crum for stepping stones of growth? Or must our mind remain a mantra
of critical voices declaring "always less-than, never enough?"*

MUSIC

Music permeates the self. Visual art and
literature can do this too, especially the musical
element in each. Words and colors make music
too. Sound envelops, passes through defenses
more readily. It is invisible like wind yet moves
emotions deeply. It is intangible like thoughts
and feelings but real in impact. Very often
deeply damaged people reach for something
musical in the therapist, and hope that the latter
will respond to something deeply musical in
themselves. At such moments, how we sound
to each other is a gateway to how we taste
emotionally.

(1999, p. 82)

WORDLESSNESS IN PSYCHOTHERAPY

I have become convinced that much of what
happens in therapy, often what is most important,

is nonverbal—permanently outside the reach of words. This in no way minimizes the use of words. There are people who storm the gates with words and try to say everything ... but in most therapeutic work, there is a tone or atmosphere or "feel" in the room that is more important. Words, after all, do not merely involve the exchange of information—they are part of the exchange of states of being. There is an osmotic aspect to therapy that must not be overlooked.

(2001, p. 4)

PSYCHOTHERAPY AS LETTING BE

It is a special letting be. It is a letting be with a supportive presence. A special supportive presence, one that values psychic life, the precious flow of subjective reality. A mixture of caring respect, respectful caring that touches the longing to grow and the need to make contact with who we are, the more that we are.

(2007a, p. 123)

* * * * *

Of course, "letting be" is not simply or only what psychotherapy is about. Not at all. But the attitude conveyed in this excerpt points to something important that should not be minimized. Too often therapists are in a hurry to alleviate symptoms, rather than take time to work with deeper injury. Society's "band-aid" approach to emotional wounds is fostered by economies of efficiency and social collusion desiring quick fixes.

Allowing a person's psyche to heal at its own pace is analogous to a river restoring its own health by being left alone with no dams impeding water flow, simply supported by nature's rhythms. Our psychic and emotional rhythms deserve non-interference from careful and care filled human support as well.

STAYING IN THERAPY

If one stays in therapy, sooner or later one comes up against what is wrong with the therapy relationship. What is wrong with the therapy relationship is not something one can easily manipulate one's way out of, short of leaving, or agreeing to lie to oneself. It is something to weep over and try to change. Oddly, trying to change the unchangeable, and weeping over inability, promotes a kind of growth. The tone and texture and resonance of personality deepens.

(1998, p. 158)

STRUGGLE

... struggle is not just a negative, something you have to slog through ... it is also a point of contact with God. The struggle has an uplifting dimension as well as a crushing dimension, partly depending on attitude as well as circumstance.

(2014c, p. 24)

LIE AND TRUTH

The great lie is we're going to live forever. The great Truth is we're living forever now.

(1998, Epigraph)

* * * * *

Some religions believe in an eternal afterlife of heaven or hell—life forever after. In this epigraph, Eigen points to the often-overlooked reality that heaven and hell are here with us now, states of being within us right now. We live with ourselves 24/7 and each moment is a "now" moment ... there are none other than now-moments. Even memory and anticipation are now-moments, capable of feeling infinitely good or bad, evoking pleasure or shame. Are heaven and hell anything other than this, experienced forever right now?

EMOTIONAL EXPERIENCE

In some way, are we always infants when it comes to emotional experience? From many lives I have chanced to be part of and many more heard about but never met, I would have to say that yes, we are infants when it comes to emotional experience.

(2014c, p. 68)

Now the truth: no one gets used to working with emotion from within. To work within emotional fields is always more than one can do. More truth: one is never up to the task. Psychically, we are babies trying to coordinate arms and legs before smooth coordination is possible. We flail along in semi-blundering fashion.

(2007b, p. 2)

IMPACT OF REALITY

The impact of reality is far greater than our ability to process it. We can't take too much reality. Our equipment simply is not up to it. If we are lucky,

persistent, patient, hungry enough for the real,
our equipment grows into the job, building more
capacity to work with what is. Nevertheless, we are
always behind the impact of the moment, at best
able to process crumbs broken off from the whole.

(2004, p. 8)

MEDICATION

I am not against a proper use of medication
but am against its burgeoning promiscuity,
which I fear depletes and retards developing a
much-needed capacity to digest feelings and use
oneself and others in nourishing ways. One might
diagnose the human condition as a disease, but
it would not be clear that medication could cure
it or that we, human beings, would know how
to use the medication we produce. One never
recovers from being human.

(2016a, pp. 136–7)

OPENNESS WITHIN CLOSED DEPTHS

A discovery for myself through life has been that
in the closed depths, there is something infinitely
open. Not just the image of one door opening
when another closes, although that's fine. But
something more, deeper, less understandable.
In the very depths of the unpacked density of the
closed, in the depths of its very obdurateness and
inaccessibility, there is an open infinity. When first
finding this, it felt miraculous, mysterious. It may

well be. But it has become something else for me with the years, part of my everyday working life, partly where I live ...

In my experience, going into density can connect with infinite openness.

(2016a, pp. 23–4)

SENSING

For me, the term "sense" has special significance. It is one of those uniting words that spans psycho–spiritual dimensions. Sense as in vital sensing. Sense as in the various senses, hearing, seeing, touch, taste, smell, proprioception, interoception, kinesthesia, all of which open worlds of experiencing, add color to life, add life to life. One could add inner sensations associated with breathing, digestion, sexuality.

Sense associated with common sense. Sense associated with meaning. Sense associated with judgment and evaluation, good sense, bad sense. A sixth sense associated with intuition, inner guidance, and direction. Sense is a term that runs through capacities and modes of experiencing. With a slight transposition, sense terms can be used for psychic taste and smell. We taste, smell and touch each other's personalities, character, tone, essence. Freud wrote of consciousness as a sense organ for the perception of psychical qualities. A sense organ that has depth as well as surface and can hardly be located simply as "consciousness."

(2016a, p. 25)

INSTINCT AND SPIRIT

Sensitivity spans many dimensions and symbolic worlds, making use of sexual sensitivity and symbolism, on the one hand, and mystical sensitivity and symbolism, on the other. The extremes can seem vast indeed but also connect and fuse in many ways, as in sexualizing God or deifying sex. Psychoanalysis teaches that sex connects with everything. Religions teach that God connects with everything. It is no surprise that psychoanalysis and mysticism have deep inner connections, if both connect with everything. Instinct and spirit are not only at war, but also deeply feed each other.

(2004, p. 16)

THE FIRE THAT NEVER GOES OUT

Is it true that we are headed for premature extinction of soul? It may look that way at times— but I feel otherwise. I cannot believe that a world that has produced Bach's music, Blake's visions, Beethoven's agonic heavens can be a spiritual crater. There are soul singers and creators now— even in psychoanalysis. Spiritual volcanoes are ready. The history of fire is not over. Singers and fires may get smaller and smaller—but that was always part of human sensation, the greatness of the past. I suspect many of us have a basic feeling of gratitude and praise for the fire that never goes out.

(2004, p. 61)

TOLERATING FRUSTRATION

Frustration modification involves tolerating tension, life building on itself, whereas evasion involves discharge, evacuation, intolerance of tensions, getting rid of ourselves. Both movements are part of our makeup and not necessarily mutually exclusive. For example, often we push away, say no, before taking in and saying yes.

(2004, p. 67)

INSOLUBLE CONFLICTS

If we are sensitive to ourselves and the world we live in, unsolvable conflicts are inevitable. At times, the best one can do is wait, let problems be, turn them over this way or that and see what happens in time. Waiting on a problem builds waiting ability. Tolerating difficulties builds tolerating ability. In psychosis there is a demand to right things totally now, a utopian vision that dooms therapeutic effort.

(2004, pp. 68–9)

DISPROPORTION WITH OURSELVES

Our need to help, to nourish is a profound and vital part of our nature. But not the only part. We would not be here today if we were not so variant. It is difficult to cognize our vast discordance, what Pascal pointed to as our disproportion with ourselves. That we are cruel killers. That we are caring lovers. That we nourish and destroy. That we are guilty, that we are guiltless. It sometimes seems that we hurt each other so that we can help each other. Is there such a thing as nourishing gestures free of wounding components? Is that, in part, what we mean by grace?

(2006, Part One)

HOW DOES CHANGE HAPPEN?

How does change happen...? I'm not sure I can say ... And in psychotherapy? What is it that draws us on, leads us on ...?

What place can sincerity or devotion have in a psychopathic world? I have a rough time with some of my patients, but overall I am devoted to them. Some are loaded with toxins, self-hate, anger. But whatever tastes I get are nothing compared to what they live. There comes a time when one no longer can blame the intrinsic pain of life on oneself or others ...

Even if we are hard put to say exactly why this happens and not that, why or how this person benefits a lot or a little, we best follow Buddha's advice and keep practicing. Keep on doing it, this mysterious process in which one being touches another and one touches oneself. As we do it something grows richer. *We* grow richer. More keeps happening. Paths, dimensions, experience open. There is no answer, only more to do and feel.

No tricks. Just working, finding, feeling, thinking, communicating, keeping at it. Sometimes it feels like we're monkeying around in the basement or sometimes working with the flow the psyche is. Psychic respiration, circulation, digestion. How a person affects another or affects oneself. Quality of attunement is only a start. It's a treacherous business. So much can go wrong anytime and if we are lucky, we work with what goes wrong. I think of Asian carpets weaving errors into art.

(2016a, pp. 142–3, original emphasis)

* * * * *

Psychic respiration, circulation, digestion mirror or parallel our physical processes necessary for life and health. Why should psychic reality be any different? The effects of chronic emotional patterns on physical health are increasingly being taken seriously, adding to knowledge about the health of our psycho–physical beings.

PSYCHOLOGICAL AMPHIBIANS

Is madness too strong a word? Would it be better to speak of alternate realities, other spaces, other concerns? We are psychological amphibians, water and land creatures. More, as ancients hint, earth, fire, water, air, all dimensions of experiencing. One of our great challenges is flow between worlds. Taoism speaks of a hinge, capacity to go back and forth,

to pass in and out of multiple realities, to value
the plethora of capacities that constitute us.

(2014d)

SURVIVING PSYCHE'S PRESSURES

The psyche can only take so much of itself. Only
so much build-up of emotion, pressure, and
tension is tolerable ...

What our nature produces can be ahead
of its capacity to process and digest. We are
traumatized by incapacity to tolerate and
work with what happens to us and within us.
Traumatized by our own emotional reality ...

Not all life is catastrophic. There is much
joy, pleasure, beauty, bliss, goodness. Yet,
catastrophe is a thread that runs through it,
sometimes more, less ...

... If we do not find ways of meeting fears that
haunt and beset us, we are in danger. We are in
danger anyway, tossed, as Taoist sages say, like
rag dolls by waves of emotional intensities with
little capacity to sustain them. Paradoxical beings
challenged to develop capacities to work with a
baffling nature. We have "successful" moments,
but it cannot be said that we know what we are
doing. Perhaps we ask ourselves to do what we
cannot do. If that is so, it is a situation worth
acknowledging and letting in. If we keep the great
unknown in the foreground, perhaps we can learn
more about what we *can* do with less belligerence.

(2014b, pp. 123–4, original emphasis)

FULL AND EMPTY

When one contrasts full–empty, one has to be careful of context. As language teaches, a person can be full of himself, too full, or full in a wrong way. To say someone is full of himself is close to saying he is full of shit. At the same time, there is fullness of inner riches, my cup runneth over. Likewise, being empty of self or having a self that feels empty has to be contextualized. It is too simple to draw a distinction between positive and negative emptiness, but that helps to get a sense of what is at stake. Creative emptiness, creative void, uncarved block, embryonic, unborn, no-thing—terms linking with potential, staying open, possibility ... On the other hand, there is the emptiness of the lost in spirit, one who is empty of life. Terms can turn many ways.

(2014c, p. 124)

ARTISTS OF THE INVISIBLE

To have a successful dream is not just to feel better, to succeed in wish fulfillment, but to nibble on what is bothering one a little more. Nibbling on what is bothering one sooner or later brings one to a nameless irritant built into life, an agony that remains invisible no matter how one names it. Exploding dream bubbles challenge us to become artists of the invisible.

(2007b, p. 28)

FAITH AND BELIEF

By faith, I do not mean belief. We literally kill each other over beliefs. Faith supports experiencing and exploration of experience. Faith is deeper than belief. Belief often functions as premature organization, closure of faith. One way that faith goes beyond belief is by enabling unknown transformations that open reality, transformations we may sense but are unable to pin down. Meditation, for example, can take us to places that have no name.

(2014b, p. 6)

Faith plays an important role in transformational processes in psychotherapy. I don't mean "belief". Belief may be a necessary part of the human condition but it tends to prematurely organize processes that remain unknown. For me, faith supports experimental exploration, imaginative conjecture, experiential probes. The more we explore therapy, the more we appreciate how much our response capacity can grow. We are responsive beings, for good and ill. Too often, our responses hem us in. We short-circuit growth of responsiveness ...

It is as if something pains us, as if life, the human condition pains us, and we try to excise the pain without knowing what it is. We grab at this problem or difficulty and attack it thinking, at last, the pain will be solved. If psychoanalysis has taught us anything, it is that we are persecuted by our own nature, which finds voice and resonance in structures of the outside world. In part, social structures, from family to state, are ways we try to organize pain, hoping to diminish, even solve it. I suspect we do not know what is bothering us. Beliefs hide this fact. Faith opens it.

(2011b, p. viii)

... the faith I write of is a critical faith, not dogmatic belief ... faith is deeper than belief ... I feel a deep faith in the heart of religions I know, but people fight over belief systems. The deep heart of faith brings us together, the belief of religious systems is territorial, aggressive. Belief functions as a defense against faith as well as a codified (often rigidified) expressive outgrowth of it. Faith as a psychoanalytic attitude is not belief so much as a more open approach towards emotional experience.

(2014c, p. 119)

AN INTIMATE PRESENCE

It is said that Buddha reached bottom, the end of it, no more to go, and it is said he never arrived. There is no end to my I don't know, no bottom. I sit in not knowing with an intimate presence, a close friend, amazing stranger, dreaded power, closer to me than I am. Some say that intimate presence is yourself, your own mind, part of inner dialogue, the Broca area, your parents. I do not say no. But something eggs me on, not quite this,

not quite that. Nothing I learn about it is quite
satisfactory. An amazing presence is embedded
in the heart's center. Infinite, intimate presence.
"Who are you?" I ask. Who or what is it? I don't
know. Yet the intimacy of Infinite Intimate
Presence is better than "knowing."

(2011a, p. 51)

EIN SOPH WITHIN

In Jewish mysticism, Ein Sof represents the
unknowable infinite mystery beyond duality,
existence, time, and space. A boundless infinite
that, I feel, is part of human personality, at least
in intimations. The God of creation, Yahweh,
emanates from divine mystery, emanations that
give birth to experience. I suspect when we try
to describe such sensations, we touch what
Winnicott (1992) calls an "incommunicado core"
linked with Ein Soph within.

(2016a, p. 1)

* * * * *

In Human Nature, Winnicott (1988, p. 132) *says of the infant:*
"*At the start is an essential aloneness. At the same time this aloneness
can only take place under maximum conditions of dependence* ..."
  Meditating on Winnicott's sense of aloneness, Eigen writes:

An aloneness that is supported by another one
does not know is there. A primary aloneness,
supported by an unknown boundless other.
To think that aloneness has in its very core a

sense of unknown infinite other. No wonder
Winnicott says so much depends on the quality
of environmental being and response. The very
quality of our aloneness depends on it.

(2009, p. 12)

Eigen extends this thought in another book:

I, personally, experience something sacred in this
core. I think Winnicott did also. Our lives tap into
a sense of holiness connected with a background
aura of infinite unknown support. That such
an implicit sense is there offers no guarantees
about how we use it ...

(2014b, p. 31)

INSIDE EYES
There is an urge to rip off mental and emotional
clothes, tear our minds out, get to the bottom
of ourselves, find something we cannot doubt
or take another view of. But as long as we have
minds, we may take another view. Flies have a lot
of outside eyes, and we have a lot of inside eyes.

(2004, p. 53)

LETTING EMOTION SPEAK
.... I read in Bion that no literal documents can
convey the affect of the session. The analyst
almost has to be a poet, an artist, for the feeling
of the session to find expression on a page. How
can what you write do justice to the emotional
truth of a session? You have to write from the

affect, let it speak. It's not a matter of literal or figurative writing. All my writings are ways of trying to get through to the reader, subject to subject, self to self, mind to mind, heart to heart.

(2007a, p. 62)

EVOCATION OF MEANING

How might psychoanalytic language be used in such a way that it carries within it an experience of the thing being described?

Bion's criteria for good psychoanalytic writing captures this:

... the criteria for a psychoanalytic paper are that it should stimulate in the reader the emotional experience that the writer intends, that its power to stimulate should be durable, and that the emotional experience thus stimulated should be an accurate representation of the psychoanalytic experience that stimulated the writer in first place.

(Bion, 1984[1965], p. 32)

Eigen's use of language to describe emotional and psychological processes blends evocative precision with rigorous mystical sensibility. He describes such tensions this way:

Poetry and religion are as hard pressed to express and explore the depth of human experience as science. The very elusiveness of so much of what we experience keeps us wondering who and what we are as well as where we are. The poet and mystic use language evocatively, although precision and rigor are necessary for evocation to succeed. It may be that the depth psychologist must also develop his own style of evocation ... The psychologist is obliged to think as clearly as possible, but it is, finally, thinking rooted in a specific sensibility. A certain tension between clarity and evocation must be maintained.

(2018b, p. 22)

INNER SCREAM

Maybe part of what needs to happen (in therapy) is to sit with the explosion, hear the SOS; listen, hear the scream. There is a scream inside ... Stay with the scream, an inaudible scream of your patient's being, perhaps your own being as well ... The scream is a sign of distress that cannot be addressed by the screaming one. A distress the adult or baby cannot solve, an unsolvable disturbance. And that is where you come in. Not that you have a quick fix, a solution. But you are prepared to stay with that scream ... sit with the unsolvable disturbance, providing a background support for something to grow over time.

(2012, p. 20)

WHAT CAN WE GIVE?

What, then, are we called on to give? We are asked to give ourselves. To give of ourselves. And for this, no one else will do. There are no

substitutes for what only you bring now, this
particular, passing forever.

(2014b, p. 3)

FAITH AS OPENING

The paradoxical result of reaching toward one's
basic madness and the traumatized self is feeling
more alive and real. The model is not control so
much as opening one's experiential field.

(Wilfred) Bion calls this opening faith ... Faith
is an open attitude that lets things register, it
is not the closed faith of a particular religious
dogma, ready to do violence to what is outside it
... The faith Bion has in mind is part of the need
sensitivity has to taste life, to feel impacts and
digest them in ways that lead to more life.

This kind of faith is an attempt not to do violence
to experience, an attempt that must fail, perhaps.
But the attitude it embodies is significant—a
caring, devotion, sincerity, respect, an imaginative
loving objectivity, a drive to do life justice, a need
to do right by experience. If taken seriously, one
possible result of this kind of faith is increased
ability to wait on each other, wait for each other ...

(2004, p. 9)

PSYCHOANALYTIC INTUITION

Psychoanalysis is, among other things, a method
of exploration. But it is necessary to reinvent
or re-envision psychoanalysis according to the

requirements of a particular situation. What is at issue is not simply growth or variation of method, but evolution of psychoanalytic intuition itself. Psychoanalysis is only as alive as a practitioner's intuition in a given predicament.

(2001, p. 85)

INFINITY, INVISIBILITY, AND EXPERIENCING

It is a paradoxical and essential characteristic of our beings that knowing and unknowing can be imbued with a sense of infinity. Almost any important area of experience can be infinitized. For example, in our dreams the sense of danger can become boundless, as can bliss ...

The sense of convergence of knowing and unknowing, together with a sense of infinity, is possible, in part, because experiencing as such is intangible and ineffable. We cannot locate a thought as we do the brain. However much we associate emotions and centers of consciousness with the body or read a soul in a face or a gesture, something invisible remains ... The basic invisibility of experiencing contributes to a sense of boundlessness that tinges our existence.

(2018b, pp. 328–29)

EXPLOITATION OF EMOTIONAL CAPACITY

I don't think feelings get digested today. There are massive social pressures to thin feelings out or eject them like missiles at or into others (other groups, individuals, parts of self). Feelings get commercialized, politically marshaled and packaged, turned into money or power, slicked up. Various electronic media and image producing machines speed and spread the resulting packages and programs, so that feelings are used for gain, a kind of widespread psychopathic exploitation of emotional capacity with resulting stunting or warping or numbing or over-excitation of the latter.

(2016a, p. 132)

EMOTIONAL ANOREXIA

Feelings nourish us. If we must cut off feelings to cut off danger, we become emotional anorexics. If we begin starving ourselves of feeling, it is a small step to become emotional gorgers and purgers.

(2001, p. 34)

ASSIMILATING OUR PRODUCTS

One part of the human condition is that our products are ahead of our ability to assimilate them. We produce thoughts, we produce products, and we produce technological knowhow way ahead of our ability to assimilate them. We produce experiences, but our capacity to digest them is far behind. So, I think that we haven't digested what psychoanalysis is producing.

An assimilation process hasn't caught up with pathways that are opening.

(2014b, p. 115)

DISTINCTION-UNION

At the same time that we are connected, or in union, with everything, we're also distinct. This balance of identification and distinction is what I call the distinction–union structure because both elements are always co-present and nourish and antagonize each other. A kind of DNA and RNA of the psyche. Each psychic act is characterized by this double tendency. And this double tendency is a unity, a system. We have all kinds of aberrations of the system, disjunctions of distinction–union, denial of one or the other. "I'm afraid of being distinct." "I'm afraid of uniting."

(2014b, p. 110)

Something of this principle, I suspect, applies to more full or void people. I think that the two tendencies, or organizations, plenitude and void, the cup runneth over and the empty cup, are crucial moments of existence. We need to live our way into both, make room for both, be less scared of either side. Fullness can be scary because of the intensity. It's too much. Void can be terrifying because you're afraid you're going to disappear, there'll be nothing, and you haven't discovered how freeing no-thing can be.

There's a dialectical, or, in Winnicott's terms, a paradoxical, relationship between these capacities, and a void person will have to develop the fullness aspect in her/his own way and the fullness person will have to develop the void aspect in her/his own way. At the same time, it says in the *Talmud*, go from strength to strength, don't play down your strength. If your strength is in the fullness area, then your job is to mine it. To work the field, farm it. Your job is to do something with what you are given. If your strength is in the void area, your job is to cultivate it. Bring it out. Let it evolve, develop, and open up to the realities that it opens for you.

(2014b, p. 112)

MORE DISTINCTION-UNION

Strictly speaking, to exist and be undifferentiated is not possible. Anything that is, must, in some way, be differentiated. Otherwise, it could not be noted, addressed, or engaged … A self with no object or reference point outside it would vanish.

(2018b, p. 150)

* * * * *

To exist and be totally merged or in union is not possible as a sustained reality. Even a yogic master in deep meditation, claiming a Samadhi of absolute oneness, achieving merger with void, divinity or the Absolute, could be asked: how might such an experience be known or marked? By one's absence? Like when we say, "I must have been asleep because I can't remember being awake?" Even within absolute union or merger, one needs a little distinction to note that unity is happening. So, neither pure merger (union) nor pure separateness (distinction) can be sustained in lived experience.

MYSTICAL DISTINCTION-UNION

Separate, yet not separate, distinct and interlacing and one—lit up as far as human capacity can bear light, limited and limitless, emanating from a source that eludes manifest knowing, a source giving rise to intimations, implicit contact.

(2014b, p. 89)

LIKE SAINT AUGUSTINE

Like Saint Augustine, my heart exclaims: in the mountains, You are there. In the rivers, You are there. In the depths or heights, You are there. In hatred, You are there. In containment, You are there. In love, You are very there. In emptiness, You are there. In loss, You will appear. In horror, I have no one else but You.

Dare I call You Self? You are closer to me than I am, closer than Self. You have made me more caring, more frightened, braver. You who are more, I am more through You.

(2013, Epigraph)

YOU CAN'T LITERALIZE THE PSYCHE

You can't literalize the psyche. You can't nail the psyche to words—she said he said—in a concrete way. "Honesty" is not enough. Psyche bursts through, catches you, and realizes itself through holes in your net. These books, like all others, overflow with psyche that letters can't contain. You can use words like bait. The fish are another matter. Water is filled with them. The fish eat the words that catch them, the words eat the fish. The fish disappear, words do too. The most important things are always left out.

(2007a, p. 62)

CONFUCIUS AND COMPASSION

Confucius says in the *Analects* that he feels like a failure. All his life, he loved the Way, spoke of the Way, tried to help others move along the Way yet he felt he never achieved it, not fully, not permanently. As an older man, he felt that he himself failed to reach the state he was advocating throughout his lifetime. My feeling is that Confucius likely lived a much better life than he would have had he not tried to live the Way. But in the end he confesses failing to do it. Now, if Confucius failed to do it, what else is there for us to do but have compassion for *our* failures. It doesn't mean we shouldn't try. But it does mean we should have compassion for ourselves in whatever state we end up in, in whatever state we find ourselves.

(2011b, pp. 102–3, original emphasis)

SURVIVING ALIVENESS

A strange world we live in where a central theme is: can the mother take the baby's aliveness and with what quality? Can we survive each other's aliveness? Can we survive our own aliveness and how? The fate of feeling depends on capacity to respond to it, an evolutionary challenge.

This highlights a circle. Where does capacity to respond to the infant's destructive force come from? From having been responded to as an infant?

(2014b, p. 27)

The basic situation is fraught with difficulties. Bion depicts an infant's seeking tendencies as too strong for its own personality—and perhaps too much for parents as well. The possibility that as a species we may be too much for ourselves is a theme that runs through Bion's work. Our task is an evolutionary challenge. Can we take ourselves? Can we take what we put into each other? Bion suggests that we cannot take ourselves unless we can take each other. At the same time, capacity to take one another is poorly evolved. We do not take each other very well. We hope that the ability to do so grows and that the capacity to support mutuality presses further into existence because of need and practice.

(2001, p. 36)

TOOL-MAKING AND REVERSAL

Tool-making is an example of how good turns into bad. Tools we make take on a life of their own, proliferate, turn against us. Planes crash or are used as weapons. Technological advances turn us into targets of lethal gadgets or poison our air and water. Communication media deform consciousness, creating information addicts, cogs in the machine of marketing mania and greed. What seems an expansion of possibilities has unforeseen consequences ...

(2005a, p. 38)

PSYCHE NEVER STOPS

A movement of becoming at the core of personality, an invitation to further realization. It is the necessary form of dramatic narrative that no climax is final, there will be more, just as no dream or thought or feeling is final. Life continues, more transformation is possible, even or especially in the most secret places, new intimacies. The psyche never stops. An orgasm that never ends, ebbs and flows, stops and starts, rises and falls, a never-ending secret in plain view.

(2018a, p. 63)

YOUR FIRST PATIENT

Everyone in this room is strong. Every single person in this room has strength or you wouldn't be here. And every single person in this room is weak, is needy or you wouldn't be interested in this field because we are all here to help ourselves. We are here to help our patients. Our patients are our proxies, our doubles. And by helping our patients, we help ourselves. We are working with our own hurt selves. And we are working with the patient's hurt self. But that doesn't mean we're not strong. We are strong.

We need to make room for this sometimes baffling mixture of strength and weakness and resourcefulness to work with both. We need to make room for our own hurt selves. We will always be hurt. We'll always need more inner support for our own beings.

The sentient being you spend most time with is you. So you are your first charge. You are your first patient because you will be your patient all your lifelong. You'll be in your own care all your life long, your primary patient. Your job is to become compassionate to this primary patient, the closest one in your care. See what support and wisdom you can manifest for this being who needs your help.

(2011b, p. 74)

A ROOT SENSE

Religious language helps bring out nuances of psychological states and psychology helps make the language of the spirit more meaningful to emotional concerns today. Each brings out possibilities of the other, since both grow from a common root: a root sense touching how it feels to be alive, the taste of life.

(2014a, Epigraph)

PARTNERS IN EVOLUTION

To constitute a living person within oneself is to constitute what is destroying this person as well. The analyst must dream what destroys

the patient's dreams, and since the analyst
may or may not be much better at this than
the patient, the analysis turns on two people
becoming partners in evolution, doing work all
humanity must come to do. In other words, part
of the long-term work involves becoming real to
ourselves and to each other and the profound
ethics this implies.

(2004, p. 32)

MANY SPECIES

We are kind of amphibian, ambidextrous,
omnivorous psychically. We live in a plethora of
experiential worlds collectively and individually.
So much so, I sometimes get the impression that
many species exist within our species, which is
one reason communication can be so difficult.
Plasticity is our bridge if we exercise it fully
enough. Our interest in life, if not thwarted or
stunted, will lead us to each other, no matter how
foreign or strange we are. We are excited, not
only threatened, by difference.

We want to understand, not just conquer each
other. We want to nourish and cultivate mutual
permeability, creative vulnerability.

(2007a, p. 13)

MAKING ROOM FOR EXPERIENCING

It is not unusual to try to talk ourselves or each
other out of experiencing by prematurely trying
to make sense of it, often a sense driven by

habitual categories that might miss what is fresh or new in the moment. In therapy, we try to build more tolerance for letting be, making room for differences, even slight differences in the perception of oneself or others. As ever, we are involved in dialectical, paradoxical work. On the one hand, sensitively exposing and working with attitudes embedded in affect and affect embedded in attitudes, moving between analysis and more nearly pure experiencing.

(2014c, p. 126–7)

"HAVE TO" THINKING

There is a loving imperative that I don't want to hurt my children more than I have to, and that I want to diminish this "have to". "Have to" thinking should be subject to systematic mistrust, an occasion for analysis. The war worth fighting is the ongoing struggle with one's psychotic self, with destructive displays of affect and thought, with a sense that I have a right to inflict my deformations on others. If I'm neurologically destined to kill my children or yours, then I am required to fight my neurology, to battle my physiology, to alter my internal environment by opposing it, by engaging it. I am required to do this and you are, too. What dictates this imperative? Simply, a sensitive sense of each other and ourselves. To employ destruction for good, an age-old calling, wish, necessity.

(2007a, p. 64)

IT FEELS RIGHT

Very often, I hear the phrase, "It feels right".
A person might use such a feeling or phrase
to justify a course of action or way of looking
at a situation, another person, and oneself. It
is hard to get used to the idea that because it
feels right does not mean it *is* right, or even if
right is relevant for the matter at hand at all.
The more I see, the more I become sensitive to
the possibility that a sense of being right can
be a signal that something destructive might be
around the corner. A sense of being right has
been used to justify going to war, a tendency
that can work on many levels, personal, familial,
within and between groups. We seem addicted to
feeling right, as if that gives us the right to assert
our position, even supremacy, over others (who
are less right or wrong).

(2014c, p. 39, original emphasis)

BLURRING COMPLEXITY

Life's equipment is blessed with normal
tranquilizing mechanisms. Babies blank out
when they are too stressed. To an extent it is
normal to soothe away bad feelings with good
ones, to substitute pleasantness (imaginary
or real) for difficulty. Feeling right is one such
natural narcotic. Like hate, it blurs emotional
complexity and uses intensity to narrow the
psychic field. To be right about everything is
promiscuous, but can we settle for less? To be

right about anything can be dangerous depending upon dosage and its use (misuse). To be right about something—our lives, our truths—to finally get it right—what can be more gratifying? What else is it all about? Yet we ought to label our sense of rightness: "High Voltage—Handle With Care."

(2005b, p. 99)

CHANTING "I DON'T KNOW"

Sometimes I think of what it would be like if the whole world, every single person, top to bottom, chanted in synchrony three words little used in high places: "I don't know." A worldwide wave of unknowing together. It takes so much effort to pretend to know and to act as if one were better than one is, more whole and knowing, and the cost to individuals and nations is high.

(2012, p. 78)

PSYCHOSIS AND CREATIVITY

Why is there so close a connection between psychosis and creativity? One reason, I suspect, is that many psychoses can only be worked with creatively. In some cases, psychosis is aborted creativity, creativity gone wrong. Something in the psychotic individual reverberates to creative responses in the other, whether the latter are effective or not ...

There are many kinds of psychosis, some more burnt out, habituated downwards, some cinders still smoldering, some strangulated aliveness waiting for resuscitation. Some patients can meet you halfway, some can hardly let a breath of life stir out of fear that it, too, will be killed or deformed, and some habitually stay in adaptations that keep one alive in narrow channels. There are many other possibilities ...

(2014c, p. 43)

"KNOWING" ANOTHER

Too often, we presume we know who the other is, we know all about him or her, and we become reactive. Our partial knowledge becomes totalized, and we saturate the space where another might be. We saturate the mystery of the other with imaginary knowing. I say "imaginary" because acting on partial knowledge as if it is total or more than it is to create a more or less make-believe other, partly real but also partly imaginary. Often, we may not be able to distinguish our make-believe other from the being who confronts us, and our imagination fuels inflammatory reactivity.

(2011a, p. 52)

LIMITS OF UNDERSTANDING

... So-called "understanding" can be suffocating. People don't like to get put in boxes. Of course, feeling understood is important in its own right and makes one feel cared for. To understand enlivens, quickens, questions, reconciles, opens.

But the understanding game is a dangerous business. Too often it is part of one-upmanship, analytic self-protectiveness, an attempt to control psychic life, cut it off prematurely.

People differ in their need for understanding. Some feel stuffed or threatened, some cared for, nourished, some feel deprived without it. Understanding can be part of the influence game, a power struggle, or a genuine light, a freeing moment. There are all kinds of relationships to understanding, all kinds of qualities and uses of it, reactions to it.

(2007a, p. 69)

THE BEAUTY OF THERAPY

One thing that is beautiful about therapy is the value it places on growing the capacity to grow. A therapist has to experience this beauty in order to have faith in it and also perhaps needs faith in order to experience the power of this beauty.

(2005b, p. 177)

THERAPY FOR THE HUMAN RACE

Reading Bion, I feel, is therapy for the human race, teaching humility in face of emotional reality, which he posits as a core of personality. If we cannot learn to work with emotional being, we remain not only hampered, but in jeopardy. And if emotional reality is inherently unknown and unknowable, at least acknowledging this situation a little, or a little more, provides some medicine against hubris and a nearly ubiquitous sense of being right, the other wrong, a wall of lies, beneficent or malignant, that offers some buffer, some raft in waves of existence.

(2014c, p. 71)

KNOWING AND NOT KNOWING

There's a taboo against not knowing in the culture. On the one hand you're told it's OK not to know—you can learn. On the other, there's shame attached to not knowing. You have to pretend to know. There is a lot of make-believe knowing. All groups are built on make-believe knowing. It's scary not to know but make-believe knowing is scarier. There's a lot of delusional clarity floating around. You might precipitate destructive events from a pretense of knowing something you don't, a pretense of omniscience. Over time, our "I don't know" in us can become friends. Your "I don't know" and you can become friends. From deep not knowing, no one is excluded. We are partners in not knowing. Letting in deep unknowing has a chance of fostering ability to wait, care and share, patience needed to live well together and be intimate with ourselves. Deep not knowing fosters new kinds of intimacy.

(2011b, pp. 82–3)

PRACTICING I DON'T KNOW

I suggest saying and feeling I don't know as a practice. Not your only practice. We need analytic thinking and intuitive thinking, left and right brain. But make I don't know part of your practice, an important part. Try it as an exercise. Who am I? I don't know. Who are you? I don't know. Practice I don't knowing.

Perhaps we should begin as children. Over time, we may get used to it.

Not knowing as part of our education, part of school, part of what we are taught.

(2011b, p. 80)

UNKNOWN INTIMACIES

Perhaps we need to practice feeling and saying "I don't know" like a musician practices scales, as part of an exercise in living. Perhaps we should begin as children. Over time ... it fosters the patience and sensing needed to live well together, to be intimate with ourselves. How is it possible to be intimate yet unknown, the deeper the unknown, the deeper the intimacy? To enter fields of unknown intimacies opens planes of existence where nothing is required other than to marvel and say thank you. More work comes afterwards.

(2011a, pp. 54–5)

CLINICAL NOT KNOWING

In practice, I often reach a deep point of not knowing, a kind of creative waiting, that shifts the ambience of the room. As time goes on, a person with me begins to sense something further, perhaps a still point of her own that is a little freeing. It is less a matter of solving problems on their own terms as shifting the center of gravity, allowing something more to grow.

(2018a, p. 73)

UNSOLVABLE PROBLEMS

An emotional problem without a "solution" or equipment to work with it exerts pressure on personality. We can try to escape the pressure or try to stay with it, to the extent we can. In either case, pressure builds. If we stay with the problem without solution and the equipment to meet it does not arrive, the problem makes demands on us, on our ability and capacities ... One thing that can happen when you stay with an emotional experience with no solution—you keep coming back to it: *it* may not get solved but *you* change, *you* grow in the process. The problem might or might not give way, but something happens to you. Batting your psyche against an unsolvable problem forces you to develop ...

(2012, p. 78, original emphasis)

WORDS TOUCHING WORDLESS

How does psychoanalysis, which we are repeatedly told is a verbal therapy, touch the infinite unknown, wordless reality? All kinds of unknown emotional transmissions occur during therapy. You do not have to be talking for them to occur. Your supportive presence, background atmosphere, tone, and texture have an impact over time that might be more important than anything you say. The combination of word and atmosphere are part of the soup, part of the ingredients.

(2012, p. 26)

CONFESSING IGNORANCE

If Socrates confessed ignorance in the face of problems related to thinking, we might begin by confessing ignorance when it comes to problems of feeling. Confession of ignorance is part of self-knowledge. Ideologies of regulation and control tend to jump the gun, since we aren't sure what it is we are trying to control and regulate or how to go about doing it. Understanding doesn't do the trick if we don't know what it is we are trying to understand. We are not sure what use to make of understanding or what to expect of it. We do not understand very much about understanding and often miscalculate what it can do.

(2005a, p. 20)

THE UNKNOWN AND UNSOLVABLE

Bion (1970, 1994) does not use the word mystery, but privileges the unknown as a basic category of experience. We act as if we know ourselves, take ourselves for granted, yet what we take to be our identities are parts of unfathomable depths. A murderer may suppose that killing another will solve a problem only to discover that difficulties

of being a psychical being continue and mount ...
Killing does not make one's problems go away ...
The urge to obliterate difficulty, the difficulty of
ourselves, is what we are up against, what we are
working with, need to work with. Respect for the
unknown and seemingly unsolvable difficulties of
ourselves is a beginning.

(2016b, p. ix)

HATRED IN RESPONSE TO DEFICIT

Our equipment gives birth to problems it cannot
handle. It is hoped that this will stimulate the
further development of equipment. In this
process a sense of deficit—acute at times—must
be lived with. At times we are like the child who
covers up his inability to read with bravado or
even delinquency. It is doubtful we will ever catch
up with ourselves or learn to read ourselves
satisfactorily. But we can keep on learning. We
can become better partners in the business of
developing the equipment (capacities) to better
work with ourselves.

Hate often molds itself along lines of deficit.
We have a sense of injury. We compare ourselves
with others and note injustices. Hate and envy
may propel equalizing activity. We may try to get
ahead of others and ourselves and outflank our
sense of deficit. However, materialistic success
may not compensate for deficiencies in our
equipment to utilize such success.

Our productions—emotional, economic, and
technological—outstrip our ability to process

them. Hatred as a chronic response to deficit may increase productivity for a time, but may narrow or diminish or harden the growth of ability to process it. I do not think we can live without hate, and hate certainly has its uses—we hate liars and injustices as well as truth—but hate does not solve the problem of the growth of equipment.

The need to feel right can be exploited to cover deficits and is often linked with hate.

Together they are elements of an immoral conscience that makes believe it knows more than it does—misuse of unconscious omniscience—to gain some spurious advantage over others, self, life, or deficit. A danger is uncontrolled inflation succeeded by unprofitable collapse, a destructive sequence—victory of the force that wipes everything out.

(2005b, pp. 98–9)

MURDER AS DELAYING TACTIC

Murder is a kind of therapy. It attempts to remove the cause of what one feels is wrong. It tries to solve problems of pain, injustice, corruption by destroying sources of stain, impurity, unfairness. Art teaches, in great detail, that problems survive murder. Stain and inequity resurface, flaws continue. Not much is added to human knowledge by murderous solutions except, perhaps, growth of awareness that murder does not achieve (for long) the results it envisions. For humanity as a whole, murder is a delaying tactic, although it may seem so final.

(2002, p. 3)

BOUNDLESS PRESENCE INSIDE ALONENESS

Winnicott points to a very important experience. A great psychic reality is at stake, a precious part of our beings we must make time for, take the time to live and to sense: aloneness supported by another one doesn't know is there. A primary aloneness supported by what I call unknown boundless other. A sense of unknown, boundless support. Aloneness has in its very core a sense of unknown infinite other. No wonder Winnicott says so much depends on the quality of environmental response. The very quality of our aloneness depends on it. A primary aloneness supported by an unknown boundless other. If you penetrate to the core of your aloneness, you will not only find yourself, there will also be this unknown boundless presence. Is it you? Is it other than you? What is it? An unknown, boundless presence at the very core of your aloneness. No matter how deep you go, you'll find it there.

(2011b, p. 20)

LOVE OF THE INVISIBLE

Job ultimately says of God, "I know you in my flesh". What kind of knowing is this? In old age, as in my youth, I love planet earth, colors, sky,

water, those close to me and many far away,
trinkets, grass, and autumn leaves, sun, moon,
music, art, depth psychology—you name it. But a
love of the invisible has grown. A love I cannot pin
down. I used to locate it in my chest. But now it is
more elusive. It can be anywhere. A sense of the
invisible keeps growing ... Love of the invisible,
part of the birth of experience that has no end.
Love of surface, love of depths, love of the visible,
love of the invisible. Wherever you are, there
is more.

(2014c, p. ix)

BEGINNING NEVER STOPS

Beginning never stops. If we take that seriously,
deeply, we begin to undergo an ethical
transformation as well as other changes. The
unknown is felt as a partner in the creativity
of our lives and meeting with others. A deeper
respect for what we do not or cannot know
underlies what we do and can know. Bion
reaches for the term "Faith" to portray the
growth of a psychoanalytic attitude, openness
to the unknown emotion of moment. Rather
than static, our approach to experience is ever
in process, a humble, caring part of our beings.
Bion humorously calls this part of the human
challenge "humbly dumbly ..."

(2018a, p. xiii)

OPENING DOORS

If you know you don't know, humility grows, and doors open to use yourself in exploratory ways ... If we know we don't know what the ultimate reality of a [therapy] session is, we are freer to use imagination, to hallucinate, feel, sense and share without putting out what we share as gospel.

(2011b, p. 59)

* * * * *

Part of the lore about D.W. Winnicott comes from his insight that giving his patients interpretations was merely a way of showing the limitations of his own knowledge.

RELIEF IN NOT KNOWING

Bion emphasizes the dread of not knowing, but it is also a relief not to have to know. Is there a god or is there not? Is there life after death or is this it? Who am I? Am I this or am I that? Who are you? Are you who I think you are? How confining would that be? When I think I do not have to know the answer to these questions, I feel relief. I can breathe more easily. To not have to know what cannot be known. To be as open as one can or dares, intermittently, if not moment to moment. To sample openness throughout a lifetime, as part of the paradoxical mix of capacities we have and are. What a relief not only not having to know, but not pretending to know.

(2011a, p. 54)

ALIVENESS AND DEADNESS

Which is worse: an individual so addicted to high levels of stimulation and tension that even slight dips in arousal level are felt as deadening, or an individual so used to a quasi-comatose or numb existence that the slightest hint of affective quickening is threatening? To be sure, one cannot tell ahead of time whether a high- or low-stimulation individual feels more alive. I have met many individuals who live high-stimulation lives, yet feel numb. At the same time, there are people who cannot take much stimulation, because every bit sets off more waves of aliveness than is bearable. The possibilities are myriad ... As therapists, we need to learn how to become better partners with our mixed or double capacity for aliveness–deadness, so that we, our patients, and this precious, dumbfounding, and maddening capacity can evolve together.

(2005b, p. 226)

PRIMARY PROCESS, PSYCHOSIS, AND PSYCHIC DIGESTION

... We also know, partly explicit in Freud, that the unconscious, the psyche and the id can be damaged (*Damaged Bonds*, Chapters 1–4). They can be deranged, they can be damaged, and if they are damaged, the primary processes are unable to play a proper role in beginning to digest experience. The psyche remains in a state of perennial psychic indigestion. The primary process is important to help initiate digesting experience. And if it is damaged, it damages experience that it is trying to digest; it adds to the damage. In psychosis, it's not simply that you go to a blissful inner realm—anyone who has worked with psychosis knows that it's not usually blissful. Maybe it's blissful for moments, but it's agonic. It's agonistic. Tormented, tortured. A tortured psyche, a tortured unconscious. You can't simply retire to some place that Jesus points to when he says, "the kingdom of heaven is within you". If you're psychotic, the kingdom of hell is within you too. You're stuck. You withdraw from the world because it's so horrible, so painful. And it is! The world is painful, but it is also painful inside.

(Daws, 2019, p. 77)

SURVIVAL NEEDS AND INTEGRITY

It may be that our minds originally grew up to fit the needs of survival. At some point in our history mind became aware of itself, and we grew into creatures who possessed a sense of emotional truth. For some portion of humanity issues of *how* we survive became as (and sometimes more) important than survival itself. The possibility of conflict between integrity and survival arose.

Bion (1970, Eigen 1986, 1992) notes that a mental apparatus that grew up to meet survival issues may be ill equipped for issues of emotional truth. The *intrinsic quality* of life, the lies we live, the collective and individual self-poisoning processes, the search for fuller, truer living—our equipment to handle such concerns may be in infancy or perhaps just being born. It may be only in the last 5 to 20,000 years that our interest in these kinds of problems has begun. This may be part of what the Bible means by dating Creation about 5,000 years ago.

(2005b, p. 98, original emphasis)

PSYCHIC INFANCY

I was saying that we don't yet have psyches – psychic capacity that can support the intensity of the thoughts and feelings we have. We do not know what to do with our mental or emotional productions. We don't know how to bring them together. So many feelings, so many thoughts, but how to process them is another matter. Our psychic means of production outstrips our capacity to assimilate what we produce. Psychic and mental digestion must always be incomplete, but maybe we can do a little better. And since our psyches are not well developed, not really up to what feelings and thoughts demand of them, we get overwhelmed. We give up on the task of growing psychic capacity that can do a better job and turn our attention to other things, like raping the environment, making war, bullying ourselves and each other ...

... Look at pain as a kind of negative example. If the psyche is too weak or underdeveloped to work with that pain, and if it is unwilling or unable to wait on its own development, it may just try to make the pain go away one way or another. It may even try to make itself go away in order to rid itself of experiences it cannot support … often violence is an attempt to make the pain of one's life go away … But the pain does not go away or stay away. It gets worse and the means to make it go away get stronger.

(2016a, pp. 136, 137)

RECONCILING LANGUAGES

We have so many languages and see things from so many perspectives. Scientific languages, faith languages, psychoanalytic languages, common sense languages, everyday languages. All of us have many languages and we're not sure how to reconcile them. Well, I'd like to say right now that we don't need to reconcile them. We need to use them. If there weren't faith languages, most of the art in the world wouldn't have happened. If there weren't science languages, we wouldn't be sitting in this building talking to each other this way right now. My feeling is that the human race needs to learn to stop the wars between different capacities, all the different languages, and begin to develop them, begin to develop each capacity as fully as possible.

(2011b, p. 10)

REAL WATER

It is part of emotional life that we can express or narrate or convey only a bit of what we feel. We do not know the whole of it. There is always some frustration built in. It is like swimming in the ocean. We can never take in the whole ocean all at once. But we do swim in part of it and the water we swim in, while not the whole ocean, is real water.

(2011a, p. 124)

IMAGINAL CAPACITY

We scare ourselves by imaginings which magnify dreads beyond comprehension. Yet our imaginal capacity is real and nourishes growth, as well as threatens it. Our very capacity to experience (think, feel, imagine, sense) can be too much. We do not know what to do with the range, color, intensity available. We translate bits of it into art, poetry, drama, mystical vision, intersubjective know-how. But it also produces wars and threat of greater wars—between individuals, groups, nations. We injure ourselves and each other in both crude and ingenious ways.

(1998, p. 18)

TRYING TO DO BETTER

... there is a seed of unquenchable optimism in our sea of pessimistic realism. Are we not catching on that it is up to us to work with the equipment we have been given, to partner our capacities, not just exploit them, to learn and keep learning about our make-up? Is that not what we have been trying to do for thousands of years, probably longer? Is that not where evolution is taking us—closer to opposing our need to murder (whether physical, economic, social or spiritual)? Closer to embracing the struggle with our make-up and trying to do better?

(2014b, p. 8)

WHOLENESS AND HUMILITY

We wreak horror on ourselves, others, and the world at large by making believe we are whole. To be whole, we break others. (It is) no accident "total" is the root for "totalitarian." Humility is missing in pretensions of wholeness.

(2005a, p. 85)

TRANSFORMATIONAL PROCESSES

Can one say, by implication, if you are seeing the same O, you are seeing the wrong O? If O is unknowable, we are speaking in figures of speech. If one feels and says "everything is the same, nothing has changed", one expresses a real state, a significant experience or way of experiencing, even if this is not possible in reality. On the other hand, if one catches on— deeply catches on—that things are in some ways changing, that transformational processes are always at work, for better or worse, one has more of a chance of experiencing areas of freedom or possible exploration in addition to a sense of the same. One can, to a certain extent, transcend one's current situation or, better, dive into it, be with it, work with it.

Doubleness, as usual, appears. Things are always changing. Things are always the same. Both sentiments expressed as states of being. Perhaps, too, one can learn to hold this doubleness and let it work on you, take you to new mixtures of familiar–unfamiliar places.

(2014a, p. 100)

TRAUMA WORLDS AND SENSITIVITY

Many try to soft-pedal the trauma world. We are told we can transcend or transform it, not get bogged down by it, emphasize the positive. You can choose between therapists who gravitate toward pain and those who deflect attention from it. But whether one makes too much or too little of traumatic impacts, stiffens against or molds around them, hardened trauma veins are there. We are caught in a vicious circle. Undigested trauma comes at us from the outside world. What we fail to make room for and work with persecutes us from within and without. Yet inside and outside reality precipitates trauma in the first place. Inner and outer life *are* wounding.

We learn that we can adjust our sensitivity, turn it up or down, so as to modulate wounds. Some of us prefer it up high, some turn it down low, with the result that communication between people with different sensitivity levels becomes difficult. Habitual unconscious sensitivity preferences govern who feels real to us and who doesn't.

(2005a, p. 52, original emphasis)

SENSING AS MULTIDIMENSIONAL

Sensing has tended to be a second-class citizen in Western epistemology, low on the intellectual–spiritual scale. It is often taken for granted, that one transcends the senses to reach deeper dimensions of intuition and spiritual development. At the same time, sensation is a field of revelation, opening worlds that enrich one's sense of living. The term "sense" is one of those uniting words that runs through multiple dimensions of experiencing: the five senses, a sixth sense, common sense, sense as meaning, and as Freud notes, consciousness as a sense organ for the perception of psychical qualities. Worlds that keep opening the more we open to them. One even may have a sense of God, a God sense with no end. We are all explorers of where head–heart–guts bring us, and much more.

The body visible is mostly invisible. Feeling touches us from unknown places or no place at all. It is not easy to pin ourselves down and undulating waves of body feeling are part of life's elusiveness, a sense including the rise and fall of spirit that is part of a rhythm of faith.

(2016a, p. 49)

ST. PAUL AND FREUD

Whereas St. Paul knew that human nature was given to sin, Freud knew that it was immersed in madness. In an important sense, Freud's entire enterprise may be regarded as an extended meditation on our response to psychic pain. He made wounded desire the cornerstone of his depth phenomenology and charted ways the hurt, fearful, angry, demanding self worked its way out or became frozen in symptoms, life patterns, and character structure ...

(2018b, p. 366)

SUBSTITUTING PLEASURE FOR PAIN

In particular, [Freud] initiated the most detailed investigation in the history of Western thought into the ways pleasure is substituted for pain. In doing so, he went too far in reducing beatific experience to mere wishful thinking. But in the process he opened up crucial vistas into the subtle nuances of the ways we live or fail to live our lies. By demonstrating the kinship between unconscious lying and madness, he both expressed and helped restructure the sensibility of our culture.

We must discriminate between the boundless joy rooted in the depths of our nature and its systematic deployment for the sake of avoiding and falsifying painful realities. Today our inherent capacity for pleasure and good feelings is systematically exploited in the commercial and political arenas. To an extent, this was always so. But the current economic manipulation of incredibly effective public media ... can arouse and structure our wish to feel good to an extent scarcely conceivable in earlier ages.

(2018b, p. 366)

QUALITY OF UNCONSCIOUS LIFE

It's not a matter of secondary processes retraining or getting better defenses or even a shift of cognitive attitudes, important as these may be. What's more important is the quality of unconscious support of life. How does the unconscious support life? How much aliveness and what kind of aliveness can the unconscious support without becoming too destructive, without caving in or blowing its fuses.

The job (of therapy) becomes more like becoming an auxiliary dreamer or dream processor to help jumpstart a person's emotional digestive system, a process in which feelings can be better tolerated, digested, part of a fuller flow, part of deep insides, not just unleashed.

(2016a, p. 132)

* * * * *

Often, when I read the word "unleashed," I imagine variants of evacuation, like acting out or displacement. Learning to grow more capacity for tolerating frustration, like tolerating many difficult feelings, becomes part of deeper self-contact, part of emotional digestion and the struggle to become a more resilient human being.

MODIFYING WINNICOTT'S USE OF OBJECT

Winnicott (1992) sought a new turn on the theme of destruction meeting environment. He depicted an infant's destructive fantasies outlasted by the environment he tries to destroy. The central case is of an infant's destructive tendencies aimed at the mother who survives destruction without collapsing, retaliating, or inducing guilt. The environment survives the baby's feelings and survives them well enough, creating a sense of reality real enough in its own right and life affirming. Winnicott associates this moment with a sense of joy in the realness of being ...

I have been forced to somewhat modify Winnicott's formulation, which I think is at once real yet also an ideal. In reality I am deficient as a therapist. My responses often are mixed, miss the mark, inadequate. I have my own versions of collapse, retaliation, anxiety, shame, and guilt induction. Yet Winnicott's formulation has helped me and through me, many people I have worked with, with a slight shift of emphasis.

My emphasis tends to involve coming through. Over and over, we come through difficulties and mishaps of our personalities in particular situations. We survive ourselves, at times with decent quality. Therapy, as so much of life, is practice in survival and quality of survival. Coming through the muddle, at times the worst. It is an ancient model, destruction and rebuilding of the holy temple, death and resurrection, rebirth rituals.

It happens in daily life hour to hour. Now one is more dead, now more alive, different qualities of deadness and aliveness. Sleeping and waking is another bit of the model. Beckett spoke of failing better. Coming through better. It may happen instantaneously but often takes a lot more time. *Waiting* and *staying with* are important. There is such a thing as creative waiting, a capacity that builds...

(2016b, pp. 5–6, original emphasis)

FIGHTING OVER DIFFERENCES

It is said that we fight over small differences. We fight over big ones too. Can we find another way to experience differences, train ourselves to be less belligerent? Sometimes I feel the human race is made of different species. Difference in sensibilities can seem so great. When I think of all the plant and animal forms I feel appreciative and wonder at the abundance of existence. I feel parallel appreciation of forms of artwork and creativity that are born from our efforts. I don't say this one or that is the truest or best but enjoy what each brings to life. There is so much to gain by differences little or great.

(2016b, p. 1)

WAITING

The word wait and reality of waiting makes a difference ...

This is something that psychoanalysis and aspects of meditation offer. Sitting with the destructive urge within rather than acting on it. Sitting as a different form of action. The dynamics of waiting in the face of destructive pulls ...

Many qualities can feed destruction, including calculation, impulse, entitlement, injustice, pleasure and/or pain, determination, cunning, chance, opportunity, vindictiveness, hallucinatory holiness.

Psychoanalysis says, sit with them all. If you can, be with them, taste and smell experience. The more you sit with experience the more happens. Threads emerge and change, new feelings, thoughts, vantage points touch you. As time goes on, tolerance for experience builds, at least a little. One even develops a taste for tasting oneself and others and not settling for "this" view and no others.

(2016b, p. 2)

BUILDING TOLERANCE AND DEFLECTING EXPERIENCE

... difficulties related to deflecting experience and the need to build tolerance for working with states like dead–dread rather than transforming them to outer realities like war, violence, reactivity, failure of responsiveness. War as a sea of deflection. How ubiquitously psyche is deflected, the war or trauma world within enacted in the outside world, perhaps in hopes it will be noticed. We have very little capacity to tolerate build-up of internal drama compared to what is needed.

An evolutionary challenge and, at this time of history perhaps a necessity, is to develop the capacity to tolerate build-up of inner experience and work with it. No simple matter. Internal and external war cannot be easily separated. Similar or overlapping processes occur in both directions. At least some of us, some of the time, can try to tolerate a little more contact with ourselves and become more observant of its workings.

(2016b, p. 56)

MAKING ROOM FOR INSUFFICIENCY

I would like to say a word for the freedom making room for insufficiency brings. I'm well aware how badly people can feel about themselves and their insufficiencies. But there can be a positive gain in tolerating and accepting limitations. Many people I have worked with, including myself, have felt the great relief a sense of limitation can bring.

When I was in my 20s and trying to storm the gates psychically and by writing, a voice told me that I would have to accept mortality in order to write. In part, this meant I would have to accept defects in my writing if I were going to write at all. My writing would have to be something less than what I wanted it to be, something less than the Great Vision.

As a young man I thought Truth could be taken by storm, by breaking through all limitations of personality, body, mind—a kind of inner commandment, thou shalt break through everything. One day, writing like mad at heightened peak and failing, a voice said I was going about it the wrong way. I should draw back, "Do what you *can*, not what you can't." The Impossible beyond remains an Eternal Allure. But on the plane of

malchut, this life, this earth—*your* life—you must
learn what you are given and what is possible.

(2016b, pp. 46–7 original emphasis)

SPEAKING AND BREATHING

… I've been speaking with God since I was a little
boy, and if Wordsworth is right, living in God even
earlier. I can't say that God hasn't answered. The
Jewish God is quite a conversationalist. Torah
says God speaks the world into being, so an
awful lot of God talk is going on …

But what if God breathes the world into being?
Ruach Elohim—the breath of God, the breath of
Life, the Holy Spirit. I suppose a dedicated verbalist
(psychoanalysis, the talking cure?) could argue that
breath was created so words would be possible.
But suppose God breathed a long time before He
felt like speaking? Perhaps God knew that once He
spoke, especially after we came along, it would be
difficult to have any peace. I think God was loathe
to open his mouth lest the beauty and power of His
words eclipse the bliss of breathing. For many, it is
easier to be awed by the fireworks of words, than
cradled and sprung by breath.

Before words and the creation of our world,
souls probably breathed freely together. Of
course, one shouldn't blame everything on
words. Animals fight, eat each other. But
words ignite fires teeth and claws can't. Myriad
creative–destructive fires. Wars of words, wills,
territories conflagrate. What would a world
without words be like?

It would be a world without a digestive system as we know it ...

There are times when it is easier to find the Tree of Life through breathing, but neither breath nor word are guarantees. Both can be wonderful channels or insidious traps. Life is everywhere and anything can tap it.

(1998, pp. 11–12)

CREATIVE WAITING

In [Anton] Ehrenzweig's book, *The Hidden Order of Art*, he delineated phases and moods of creative work (Freud placed great emphasis on mood in creativity). One moment you might feel like a god scanning great vistas from thrilling heights, the next feel that the work is shit. He writes of the importance of endurance, going through the various moods and phases, letting work build. In one passage he described Picasso sitting for hours staring at a work in progress, not knowing what to do next, emphasizing the importance of waiting. One can apply this to the importance of creative waiting in therapy sessions as well. Levinas (see Eigen, *Emotional Storm*) writes of the importance of creative waiting at the edge of impasse and evolution. In politics perhaps, more waiting, fewer wars.

(2014c, p. 46)

AM I ALIVE NOW?

Bion's expression or notation I want to bring out is F in O ... Faith in O. Bion writes it with a capital

F. It's a radical expression. How can we have faith in a reality we don't know? And why should we? It (O, reality, ultimate reality) is going to destroy us. It created us and it's going to destroy us. Processes that give life die out. I suspect for Bion the question is not whether I'm going to die but am I going to live? Do I know I'm here? Am I here now and with what quality? When I'm walking down the street, am I walking down the street? Who is walking, how much of me is walking? Where am I when I'm walking? Right now I'm giving this talk. Am I wholly here? Am I here with my whole being? Am I giving what I can? Am I alive? Is this talk alive? Does it quicken your aliveness? So the question isn't "Am I going to die?" I am going to die and not too long from now. The question is "Am I alive now?"—and what would that mean, to be alive now? That's the real question.

The idea of faith for Bion has something to do with being alive now. Am I alive now no matter what the reality is? Am I living my reality, whatever it is, whatever it does? No matter what reality does to you, no matter what it brings?

(2011b, p. 62)

SMILE AND SCREAM

Bion's writing ... provides pictures of psychic trauma taken in therapy sessions, soul deformations, hopes that feed on ruins. Variations of a scream that runs through life.

We are that scream and much more. But when the smile comes, the scream does not stop. The smile that grows out of the scream is not the same as the screamless smile, one that makes believe no scream is there.

(2005a, p. 51)

UNEVEN EVOLUTION

Consciousness is hard to support. Bion brings out how intensity of experience is hard to support. Psychic life is hard to support. We have evolved unevenly. We evolved in such a way that we can have experiences of great intensity but lack the equipment to support them. Our experiential products are ahead of ability to digest them. It is as if what our personality produces is too much for us. Our experiential capacity is too much for us, too much for itself ...

The problem of lacking support for our experiential capacity marks a more general difficulty than pinning our problems on sex or aggression, although the latter are not problem free. We need to meditate on our insufficiency in the face of our own capacities rather than blame one or another of the latter for our problems. Blaming sex and aggression distracts us from the unevenness of our evolution, our not knowing what to do with ourselves. We seem to have a blaming propensity that is contagious: it is your fault, it is my fault, it is its fault, assigning simplified causality when situations are imponderably complex and tangled. Maybe it is just us and our particular unevenness of evolution that we cannot take too much of. We have to learn how to partner ourselves, even if it takes thousands of years ...

(2012, pp. 49–50)

EXCITATORY POWERS

The nineteenth century saw an explosion of literary–philosophical images and ideas clustering around an excitatory power. A restless will to live (Schopenhauer) that cannot be satisfied and often results in evil acts to further its aims, the will to power (Nietzsche), and for some a creative power (Emerson, Wordsworth, Coleridge) that shapes existence. A sense of upsurge that can work for good or ill, partly depending on how they are met and shaped. Surges that, too often, we are helpless in face of as they toss us like rag dolls (a Taoist phrase) in the wind. The idea of control becomes something of a fetish when we cannot even name what drives us.

(2016a, p. 33)

CONTROL AND IMPULSE

Control alone is not the answer. It simply does not work well enough. For something like generative self-restraint to develop, a deeper field of psychic possibilities must form the background of one's being. The model of control that has dominated society so long promotes warp rather than warmth. Neither control nor impulse indulgence nor their fusions is the answer. We need to get outside the box of that model and let the psyche grow. We can do better than becoming impulsive, angry adults, good one moment, mad the next.

(2021, p. 12)

FAITH AND CATASTROPHE

Some of my focus in writing about Bion has been on faith in relation to catastrophe, a basic Kabbalistic theme. One can find in Bion's descent into destructive aspects of madness a faith process, perhaps related implicitly to sparks of transformation and perhaps, even more deeply, no sparks at all, a null dimension, no dimension, in which everything has been nulled.

One finds through Bion deepening dialectics between faith and catastrophic aspects of personality, one eye on destruction and another on faith in the face of destruction, perhaps an impossible faith, a faith in the face of all destruction of faith that, nevertheless, is part of transformation. Aspects of Kabbalah emphasize sparks trapped in catastrophic realities in need of redemption, restoration. There is no place you can go where there are not hidden sparks in need of liberation. Wherever you find yourself, there is work to be done. Wherever you find yourself with a patient, you have to go.

(2014b, p. 101)

FAITH AND DESTRUCTION: BOTH ARE DEEPER

I think of Winnicott wanting to be alive when he died, faith deeper than destruction. I want to make a double formulation: faith is deeper than destruction and destruction is deeper than faith. I want them as one thing. Faith deeper than destruction; destruction deeper than faith. There can be no faith after the Holocaust. Yet there is, faith deeper than the Holocaust, yet the Holocaust is deeper than faith. It is just the way it is, if you can find it. It is not one way, it is not the other. It is both ...

(2012, p. 45)

TOWARD DREAMING'S REACH

We sleep not only to dream, but to allow contact with places dreaming cannot reach, that reach toward dreaming. Bion suggests one reason sleep is essential is to make possible emotional experiences that the personality cannot have while awake. Sleep enables experience outside the reach of waking and dreaming, to move towards dreaming's reach. This coheres with the Hindu saying that everyday life is the past, dreaming is the present, and dreamless void the future.

Shall we call this a wordless, imageless unconscious, a portal through which our lives are fed impalpably and ineffably by experience that accesses us in dreamless sleep? As though God or nature or evolution has safeguarded something from our use of it, a special form of contact that we cannot ruin with our controlling narratives, or our lust for power, or our fears, which gains access to us when our ordinary focus and selective attention, even the foci of our dreams, are out of play. A contact that accesses us when we are not looking. How can something touch us if we are not aware of it? An aporia that marks our existence, our plasticity, perhaps marks us with a sense of mystery.

(2014b, p. 2)

KABBALAH AND PSYCHOANALYSIS

The two have many points of convergence ... both are preoccupied with catastrophe and faith ... both are preoccupied with infinity and intensity of experience. Both are preoccupied with shatter and the possibility of bearing and growing the kind of psyche that can work with the dimensions sensitivity opens. Both are preoccupied with ontological implications of the Unknown and the importance of emotional life ...

For many, a sense of infinity interweaves with everyday life. They are part of each other, one reality. This interweaving has been part of my life ever since I can remember and helped make my life meaningful beyond words. Sometimes, I picture individuals and humankind as a whole as a mansion with many rooms, many of which we may never enter. Perhaps this is one source of dreams of houses or apartments that show us more rooms than we imagined. We often need support, permission to occupy some of these

unknown spaces, to enter creative relationship
with the more we did not know we were.

(2012, pp. x, xii)

LIGHT AND FAITH

There are many gradations of light experiences,
spectrums from small inner flames to the great
light without location. Some version of light might
or might not appear in sessions ... much therapy
goes on in the dark but once light is experienced
it's like a compass or orienting point from which
faith arises, a sense of faith hard to undo. It
is the simple struggle of faith that is often the
nitty-gritty reality of sessions. Faith may be a
remnant of light, but keeps on working in the
dark, often "blind," with hidden night sensors.
The faith of darkness ...

... The light itself is indestructible. But your
approach to it can be destructive ... As Jung
pointed out, people use spiritual and creative
capacities for all kinds of motives ... How one
relates to an experience can be as important as
the experience itself.

(2016a, p. 130)

INVAGINATION

Mystics speak of going through many doors, worlds,
gates. Beatrice in Dante's heaven goes from one
heaven through another. Heaven keeps opening.
Invagination is often an implied image. In my early
twenties, after a physical intervention by a somatic

therapist, he asked how I felt and I spoke the truth: "I feel like a vagina." My whole body became vaginal. His paranoid aspect came to the fore and said, "How do you know how a vagina feels?" At that moment, in my experience, I was one.

A vaginal self, a vaginal body. A Lacanian might say imaginary vagina. One could give a gender analysis and rake me over the coals for my biases. What can I say? In my mind, my body— vagina. Hallucination? Can the body hallucinate? Yes, it can. Was it hallucinating then? At the moment, I didn't care. It was wonderful.

(2014b, pp. 77–8)

SHAME AND GRANDIOSITY

Shame triggers grandiosity, grandiosity blots out shame. A feeling of godliness lifts us, a sense of lowliness keeps the balance, an inner seesaw. How to work with capacities, learn to use them as they use us and develop together …

… Adam and Eve, after eating of the tree of knowledge (K), experience shame and nakedness … Yahweh asks: "How do you know you are naked?" Adam: "The woman and I ate of the tree and I know."

An inextricable combination of high and low—ashamed of what is below because of K above, higher–lower loaded with attitudes and judgments, partly opening, partly closing experience. Aristotle's "active reason" (Super-K) leaves us with shame for everything below it.

Capacity snobbery: Each capacity above looks down on ones below it. Another possibility is capacity partnership: each appreciating the contributions the others make as well as its own. There is a delusional aspect to "hierarchies."

(2016a, 66–7)

SUPPORT FOR DREAMING

What supports a dream supports a person. The ability to create a dream, to see an experience through, to process affects, to support a self—such generative work can suffer immense degradation. Damaged bonds damage unconscious processing. Unconscious processing tries, in part, to work with its damage. Such a circle can spiral—damage adding to damage. What damages a dream damages a person.

Therapy offers a potential bond to support the growth of unconscious processing. Unconscious processing is to the psyche what air or blood flow is to the body. Therapy affirms the reality of unconscious processing and helps to jump-start or reset the latter. We need a somewhat self-healing unconscious, but once the latter becomes self-damaging, we need another's unconscious to right things. Therapy provides a kind of auxiliary unconscious until one's own gets the hang of it.

(2001, p. 27)

OBJECT SEEKING AND PROJECTIVE IDENTIFICATION

For Freud it was common sense that mothering aims at alleviating baby's distress. Ferenczi depicts the mother taking the edge off the death drive and reconciling the baby to life. Bion picks up this thread and amplifies Klein's notion of projective identification as a medium for building the sense of contact. Successful projective identification sustains the sense that human contact is necessary and possible. It supports hope.

So often psychoanalysis emphasizes frustration and break of object contact as crucial for building a sense of reality and capacity for symbol formation. It is important to balance this with emphasis on the actual presence and work of the object in supporting an infant's sense of reality. A parent may be hard pressed and bewildered by infantile distress, but without a worthy try, the specter of falling into unreality gains power.

The basic situation is fraught with difficulties. Bion depicts an infant's seeking tendencies as too strong for its own personality—and perhaps too much for parents as well. The possibility that as a species we may be too much for ourselves is a theme that runs through Bion's work. Our task is an evolutionary challenge. Can we take ourselves? Can we take what we put into each other? Bion suggests that we cannot take ourselves unless we can take each other. At the same time, capacity to take one another is poorly evolved. We do not take each other very well. We hope that the ability to do so grows and that the capacity to support mutuality presses further into existence because of need and practice.

(2001, p. 36)

OUR DRIVE FOR PSYCHOPHYSICAL NOURISHMENT

Bion suggests that our very drive for psychophysical nourishment is projected into the other, that it needs support from the other for sustenance ... The notion that we are dependent on what happens to us in another person leads to a field of experience that requires careful attention ...

...Seeking and projecting go together. Seeking is part of the projecting personality. Seeking and projecting constitute a kind of drive to communicate self and touch reality. One reaches into outer space to find the inner space of another person ...

One thing that gets projected into the object is the baby's object-seeking drives. The very urge to be with another enters the other, seeks another to go into and be part of. One goes into another to create a response, to have a place in another person, to be part of someone's life. One needs the other's thoughts and feelings for one's own psychic nourishment. This level of interpenetration is deeper than issues of control ...

In order for object-seeking feelings to thrive, or even feel real, they have to be projected into another who works with them. The drive to make contact with the other needs to find the other's insides and stimulate thought, feeling, imagining. One needs to feel who one is elaborated in the mind of another. This is a little like the mother bird beginning the digestive process for the baby, only here we are speaking about the transmission and digestion of feelings involved with one's sense of being ...

... If the projecting personality cannot hit paydirt, it cannot develop. It may stagnate, grow in warps, suffer deformation. Life goes on in strangulated, sometimes determined ways. One may become passive or die out, but one may also (perhaps in circumscribed ways) become a monster. In everyday living, our monster selves often baffle us, interacting in seamless ways with our benign and well-formed aspects. By the time we awaken to ourselves, we have an entrenched sense of being excluded/included with regard to the desire of others, partly as a result of whether and how we found our way inside another and what became of us there ...

... But what if the baby is thrown back on itself, meets a wall, or more anxiety or hostility? What if, to use Bion's locution, the object is intolerant of projective identification? What if the caregiver cannot let the baby's feelings affect her or reacts destructively? What if the worst a baby can feel cannot get into another person for modification or psychic reworking? What if the other person refuses the input, evacuates it, cannot bear it, or does not have equipment to process it? What if the baby's feelings have nowhere or very hurtful places to go?

(2001, pp. 63,66)

INTOLERANT OBJECT AND MURDEROUS SUPEREGO

The search for help meets an intolerant object that becomes a model for "self-help" (i.e., intolerance of self, self-murder). The need to communicate reaches an anxious, hostile environment and learns that communication is impossible or dangerous. One's attitude towards communication becomes negative, cynical, or worse ...

(2001, pp. 36–7)

A result of object-seeking meeting an intolerant object (intolerant of projective identification) is dread of dreaming or the incapacity to dream or relate to dreams ... Bion's diary entries ... are concerned with the destruction of the capacity to dream. The capacity to dream is allied with the capacity to feel and process feelings ...

... The capacity to be nourished by life (and to nourish life) are wounded at the root, if one is too terrified to dream what must be dreamt, if one dare not dream the object that stops dreaming.

The object that cannot be dreamt can be partly described as a "murderous superego" (Bion, 1992, 1994, p. 37), made up of the object's failure to support projective identification, the collapse of object seeking tendencies, magnification of the horror of not being able to reach another's insides with one's own, reaching only traumatizing outsides ...

In such a ghastly scenario, personality comes under dominance, more or less, by an anti-feeling, anti-dreaming, anti-psyche tendency, which includes the intolerant object magnified and further distorted by traumatized/traumatizing emotional intensity. Personality becomes intolerant of itself. Emotional processing is jammed. Rise of emotion becomes a signal to shut down. Bits of hallucination, frozen and strangulated feeling, menacing or barren thoughts coagulate into impacted residues of shock.

(2001, pp. 36–8)

SPARKS

I have heard Rebbe Menachem Schneerson say, "Wherever you find yourself, no matter how desolate or meaningless a place, there is work to be done, sparks to be freed." I might add, sparks to be mined. Wherever you are, there are sparks to be mined. Sparks of life to be released in whatever place you find yourself, sparks to be experienced, worked with, created—transformative moments … There is a hidden spark everywhere. Wherever you are means "psychically", the "place" you are living your life, the feel of your life. Whatever your psychic space might be—despair, rage, love, hate, deadness, fear, joy—wherever you are, a spark is waiting for you, for you alone, because only you can contact, distill, release, explore, and be a vehicle for your unique set of sparks. Sparks right now in a process of creation. No one can do it but you, because the sparks you are involved with are creating your own being, coming into existence with your own life.

(2012, pp. 11–12)

WHAT IS FAITH?

What is faith? Not a question I can answer but I am poor at answering many questions. How

can I write about something without knowing
what it is? Yet it is, at least, so I feel. But faith
is more than feeling, at times not even feeling.
A felt sense, but not just a felt sense. A mode
of cognition? A mode of experiencing? Part of
the atmospheric condition of psychic being that
helps support the work of other capacities?
Premonition? Intimation?

In *Faith and Transformation* (2011b) I
distinguish faith from belief. Too often, I find
belief killing faith. People fight over beliefs,
my belief vs. your belief. Faith as structured
by belief systems that bring people together,
create chasms, turn people against each other. I
would like to distinguish faith from the way other
capacities try to organize it.

We might say faith spans many dimensions.
Natural faith, religious faith, faith in life, in
oneself, in others. Faith vs. cynicism. Possibly
even cynical faith. Sometimes I picture faith as
a kind of generic emptiness which can assume
many guises, many colors, fuse with all kinds of
identities and ideologies. Is nationalism a kind of
faith or anti-faith, a defense against faith? A way
of organizing life so as to miss the essential life
of faith, to miss one's encounter with faith?

Rainbow of faith, hope, care. The fact of color
that brings wonder and joy. Color thrills us. Have
you ever felt color running through your body,
permeating you? Like sound? Music?

What is it color and music try to express if
not a sacral sense that binds us to being and

takes us beyond it, through it? Keats: spirit ditties of no tone. Yeats: soul claps its hands and sings. One hand clapping, thunderous, electric no-sound, just so. Where is faith? Do you see it in fish swimming in a stream? Or perhaps just the stream itself? Is it in the cracks, the pores? Where is it not, often is asked. But, in real life, we find many places that seem to sink it, poison it, maim and, yes, kill it. Can faith die? Are there conditions in which it cannot be born? Does the human spirit die or fail to be born?

Naïve faith, sophisticated faith, critical faith. Faith with infinite dimensions and no location at all. Where is it hiding? I want to say we are living in it but I cannot speak for everyone.

"Love God with all your heart, with all your soul, with all your might." To live in this place. "The Place"—*Hamakom*—a Hebrew name for God, associated with freedom. Love God with all you are—does that come close to saying what faith is? Faith unites, binds, frees? There is a faith that aches to get closer and closer, a faith that aches to be born.

Life lives in faith, faith permeates life, every single cell. That does not exclude faithlessness, no-faith, the empty bottom.

(2014b, pp. xi–xii)

THERAPY AND UNCERTAINTY

Therapy goes on in a kind of darkness. Its method requires faith. Therapist or patient may cut a fruitful project off because short-term results are lacking, or go on and on after reaching the point of diminishing returns. In the former, one needs faith to continue; in the latter, one needs faith to stop. Such quandaries highlight the fact that uncertainty is an important part of therapeutic experience. How one grows in relationship to uncertainty is a key index of therapeutic outcome.

(1992, p. 3)

STAINLESS LIGHT AND STAIN OF LIFE

(Bion) speaks of the stainless light and the stain of life. Thus the meaning of wounded nourishment undergoes twists and turns. The light is nourishing, indeed. But so is the stain of life. Both intertwine in nourishing, devastating ways. One may cling to the Light in the face of daily injuries or cling to everyday wounds and triumphs and mock the Light. But it is also possible to open oneself, to whatever extent one can, to the play of dimensions that constitute experience and ways they spontaneously arrange themselves. To some extent—we do not know to what extent—such a capacity develops by using it.

(2001, p. 40)

FRUSTRATION MODIFICATION AND EVASION

Bion contrasts frustration modification with frustration evasion. In frustration evasion, the psyche cannot tolerate itself, gets rid of itself, it cannot support its own tension. In frustration modification an attempt is made to evolve the capacity to process feelings.

(2018a, p. 3)

HALLUCINATORY MURDER

A practical question, an ethical one. When you make an assertion that might be costly to another person (injure sensitivity), think first, "How am I hallucinating? What truth am I hallucinating? What other am I hallucinating?" Nothing is a better index of hallucinatory murder than the sense of being right.

Yes, it is important to stick up for what you believe is right. You must fight for what you believe true, if necessary. But remember, as you do, those who have been maimed, tortured, extinguished in the name of truth and right.

One might not solve this knot but one can spend more time wondering.

(2018a, p. 7)

QUALITY OF LIFE

The importance of power, money and ideology slants our sense of the human. Ambition helps make us strong, gets us places, and I wouldn't minimize its contribution to vitality and well-being. But it also leaves us truncated, suspicious, resentful, angry, ready for battle ...

... Quality of life includes emotional quality, personal quality, quality of character. Materiality (i.e., money) is judged in terms of what it adds or takes away from the quality of felt existence, the good we put it to.

(2005a, pp. 14–15)

COMMON SENSE AND VISIONS OF THE IDEAL

In optimal circumstances, common sense and the vision of the ideal feed and balance each other. Either alone may be destructive. A fertile tension exists between them. Our ability to tolerate this tension is variable. We try to simplify our situation by becoming too prosaic or poetic. We need to realize that it is natural to zigzag between polarities.

(1992, pp. 50–1)

SELF AS FAMILY

The sense of self is variable. Self is a family, a community of voices. Sensitivity sours, rigidifies, or becomes sticky without proper exercise. A baby's smile is as spontaneous as a cry. Joy and Faith are as basic as fear, suspicion, and outrage. Our basic sensitivity takes many forms, draws on diverse sources, takes many turns. It is subject to shattering, recovery, and reshaping processes, for better and worse.

(1992, p. xviii)

WARS WITHIN AND WITHOUT

I sometimes wonder if wars between parts of personality and wars between groups of people will diminish together.

(2018a, p. 61)

A DEEPER LOVE

The world has outlasted, and will outlast, all of us. It is still going after atom bomb blasts that should not have happened. There have been worse times in history, yet I am not sure I have ever lived through a crazier moment of abrasive fragility. Tension between self-hate and self-love increases. Some feel it intensely. In others it works invisibly or, as Freud suggested, through disguises, causing so much damage in so many. We are more than compliant–defiant beings. Can we, little by little, discover ways to offset self-hate with deeper love? Not the self-love of egomania, which tramples others and damages oneself as well. There is another love, deeper love, that helps, or tries to. We have a deep need—but I cannot quite say what it is. Faith is part of it, but it is much more.

(2018a, p. 22)

DEAR READER,

When I first encountered Dr. Eigen's writing, my excitement was such that I felt I must travel to New York to spend some time getting to know him. I managed to do so on many occasions over several years before the Covid pandemic hit. During each visit in those early years, we would spend some time talking about his latest book, while I caught up with his early work. I remember often exclaiming "Are you aware of all you've accomplished for psychology?! You do realize you've really done it, don't you?!" To which he would look a bit puzzled and say: "You keep saying that... but what is it I have really done?" At the time, any response I could come up with seemed woefully insufficient. Well, I'm happy to say that this book you are now holding finally conveys an adequate answer to that question.

The extracted moments of wisdom compiled herein feel a little like "wisdom-honey," even as they also address humanity's most difficult and destructive challenges. I hope the reader has been able to gather some nourishment from these various bits of honey. Occasionally, I have found some tastes of honey can reverse themselves, become flowers again, and continue to pollinate within. To paraphrase the poet Rilke: we are bees of the invisible. We collect the honey of the visible, to store it in the great golden hive of the invisible. Much that is important within these pages remains invisible and even inaudible, compelling those with a surfeit of care to develop and practice with new sorts of eyes and ears. Growth of capacity is a lifelong process. Growth of societal and world capacity seems to require thousands of years of effort, with an ever-present expectation of "failing better."

Tensions and conflicts of the many within one rubbing up against what is common within all have a long and difficult history. We are only at the beginning, and the full meaning and import of Eigen's thoughts and formulations (e.g., his distinction–union structure—process; his rhythm of faith) have yet to be unpacked and used productively. While many of the quotes in this book convey what in our nature and development we are up against, it is in service to the future, as well as to ancestors, that we keep trying. Just as it is in service to individuals and families that psychotherapy and psycho-analysis both "struggle with life to release life, to make life better."

Whenever I visited Michael Eigen at his Manhattan office, I would walk by a building around the corner whose façade was engraved with words from Micah in the Old Testament, imploring us to do what is just, to love kindness, and to walk humbly with our God. Such a life of service has been well modeled by Eigen, who continues to work late into his eighth decade. In our era, the balance between serving others and being self-serving has gone wildly astray. My hope is that the invisible and inaudible messages within these pages might offer some pathways toward restoring that balance.

Bagai, R. (2023). *Commentaries on the Work of Michael Eigen: Oblivion and Wisdom, Madness and Music*. London: Routledge.

Bion, W. R. (1965/1984[1965]). *Transformations*. London: Karnac.

Bion, W.R. (1970). *Attention and Interpretation*. London: Karnac.

Bion, W.R. (1992, 1994). *Cogitations*. London: Karnac

Daws, L. (Ed.) (2019). *Dialogues with Michael Eigen: Psyche Singing*. London: Routledge.

Eigen, M. (1992). *Coming Through the Whirlwind*. Wilmette, IL: Chiron Publications.

Eigen, M. (2004[1993]). *The Electrified Tightrope*. London: Karnac.

Eigen, M. (1998). *The Psychoanalytic Mystic*. London: Free Association Books.

Eigen, M. (1999). *Toxic Nourishment*. London: Karnac.

Eigen, M. (2001). *Damaged Bonds*. London: Karnac.

Eigen, M. (2002). *Rage*. Middletown, CT: Wesleyan University Press.

Eigen, M. (2004[1993]). *The Electrified Tightrope*. London: Karnac.

Eigen, M. (2004). *The Sensitive Self*. Middletown, CT: Wesleyan University Press.

Eigen, M. (2005a). *Emotional Storm*. Middletown, CT: Wesleyan University Press.

Eigen, M. (2005b). *Psychic Deadness*. London: Karnac.

Eigen, M. (2006). *Guilt in an Age of Psychopathy*. Available at <http://www.psychoanalysis-and-therapy.com/human_nature/eigen/part1.html>

Eigen, M. & Govrin, A. (2007a). *Conversations with Michael Eigen*. London: Karnac.

Eigen, M. (2007b). *Feeling Matters*. London: Routledge.

Eigen, M. (2009). *Flames from the Unconscious, Trauma, Madness, and Faith*. London: Karnac.

Eigen, M. (2010). *Eigen in Seoul: Volume One, Madness and Murder*. London: Karnac.

Eigen, M. (2011a). *Contact with the Depths*. London: Karnac.

Eigen, M. (2011b). *Eigen in Seoul: Volume Two, Faith and Transformation*. London: Karnac.

Eigen, M. (2012). *Kabbalah and Psychoanalysis*. London: Karnac.

Eigen, M. (2013). *Reshaping the Self*. London: Karnac.

Eigen, M. (2014a). *A Felt Sense: More Explorations of Psychoanalysis and Kabbalah*. London: Karnac.

Eigen, M. (2014b). *Faith*. London: Karnac.

Eigen, M. (2014c). *The Birth of Experience*. London: Karnac.

Eigen, M. (2014d). Yahoo message board comment. May 3, 2014.

Eigen, M. (2016a). *Image, Sense, Infinities, and Everyday Life*. London: Karnac.

Eigen, M. (2016b). *Under the Totem:, In Search of a Path*. London: Karnac.

Eigen, M. (2018a). *The Challenge of Being Human*. London: Routledge.

Eigen, M. (2018b). *The Psychotic Core*. London: Routledge.

Eigen, M. (2021). *Eigen in Seoul: Volume Three, Pain and Beauty, Terror and Wonder*. London: Routledge.

Winnicott, D. W. (1988). *Human Nature*. New York: Shocken Books.

Winnicott, D. W. (1992). *Psychoanalytic Explorations*. C. Winnicott, R. Shepard, & M. Davis (Eds.). Cambridge, MA: Harvard University Press.

Index

For Product Safety Concerns and Information please contact our EU
representative GPSR@taylorandfrancis.com
Taylor & Francis Verlag GmbH, Kaufingerstraße 24, 80331 München, Germany